EXPLORER

GW00359600

Abu Dhabi

MINI VISITORS' GUIDE

www.explorerpublishing.com

Abu Dhabi Mini **Visitors'** Guide 3rd Edition
ISBN – 978-9948-442-99-8

Copyright © Explorer Group Ltd 2010
All rights reserved.

All maps © Explorer Group Ltd 2010

Front cover photograph: Sheikh Zayed Grand Mosque – Victor Romero

Printed and bound by
Emirates Printing Press, Dubai, UAE

Explorer Publishing & Distribution
PO Box 34275, Dubai, United Arab Emirates
Phone (+971 4) 340 8805   Fax (+971 4) 340 8806
info@explorerpublishing.com
www.explorerpublishing.com

Welcome to the *Abu Dhabi Mini Visitors' Guide*. This mini marvel has been passionately prepared by the same team that brought you the *Abu Dhabi Explorer (Live Work Explore)*. Written entirely by residents, and perfect for visitors, you'll find all you need to make the most out of your time in this interesting emirate – whether you're looking for the top restaurants, the most stylish shops or the best cultural spots.

Abu Dhabi is a thriving, cosmopolitan capital in the heart of the Middle East. Its dynamic blend of modernity and heritage, eastern and western influences, and natural and manmade attractions makes it a fascinating place to visit. Explorer brings you insider knowledge of the sights and sounds of this exciting emirate from the architectural splendour of the Sheikh Zayed Grand Mosque to the high octane excitement of the Formula One Grand Prix race at Yas Marina Circuit. Beyond the capital there are impressive destinations to explore from the green oases of Al Ain to the awesome deserts of Al Gharbia.

For more information about Abu Dhabi and the UAE, plus up-to-the-minute events and exciting new releases from Explorer Publishing, log onto www.liveworkexplore.com, where you can also give us your own take on this unique city.

The Explorer Team

Welcome...

Contents

Essentials

Welcome To Abu Dhabi

From its origins as a centre for pearl diving and fishing, Abu Dhabi has developed at breakneck speed to become a truly 21st century destination.

As the capital of the United Arab Emirates, this is one of the world's most prosperous and rapidly developing cities. In little over half a century it has seen a dramatic transformation from a small Bedouin settlement to a thriving business and tourism centre of global stature.

The UAE sits on the north-eastern part of the Arabian Peninsula, bordered by Saudi Arabia to the south and west and by Oman to the east and north. The country is made up of seven emirates of which Abu Dhabi is by far the largest, occupying over 85% of the landmass. There are two major cities within the emirate: Abu Dhabi and Al Ain, which lies at the foot of the Hajar Mountains on the border with Oman.

The island city of Abu Dhabi is a lush, modern metropolis which has so much to offer new visitors with its tree-lined streets, futuristic skyscrapers, huge shopping malls and international luxury hotels. The city is surrounded by the sparkling azure waters of the Arabian Gulf which present a striking contrast to the large parks and green boulevards that spread across the island.

Built on a grid system running from a central 'T', the city is easy to navigate. The 'T' is formed by the Corniche (p.72), which runs along the end of the island furthest from the mainland, and Airport Road which runs the length of the island. Roads parallel to the Corniche have odd numbers (the Corniche is 1st Street) and roads running vertically have even numbers (Airport Road is 2nd Street, with 4th Street, 6th Street, etc. leading off to the east, and 24th Street, 26th Street, etc. to the west).

With much of the interior of the emirate comprising desert, including part of the spectacular Rub Al Khali (Empty Quarter), or sabkha (salt flats), many visitors are surprised by how green the cities are. The combination of high temperatures and inhospitable terrain limits the variety of natural fauna and flora but the Abu Dhabi authorities are working hard to 'green' the urban landscape. Everywhere you look you'll see manicured lawns, pretty flowers and an abundance of palm trees which are maintained by an army of workers.

Over the next few pages you'll discover Abu Dhabi's rich cultural history, which should prove to be a good framework for your trip. There is plenty of advice about what to do when you first arrive and where to go when you are ready to explore. For tips on the must-do activities during your stay see p.22. The Exploring chapter (p.80) highlights the key areas and their cultural highlights including the museums and heritage sites. Sports & Spas (p.154) gives you the lowdown on some of the best activities in the emirate – from watersports to decadent spa treatments. The Shopping chapter (p.180) is a handy guide to the various souks and malls and includes tips on where to pick up those key buys (p.186). When it's time to fuel up, turn to the Going Out section (p.208) for the best restaurants, clubs and bars in the city.

Culture & Heritage

The rich cultural legacy of this region runs alongside its innovative architecture, multicultural community and rapid growth.

Settling On Abu Dhabi Island

Despite the opportunities for fishing and grazing, it was not until the discovery of freshwater, in 1793, that the ruling Al Nahyan family, based in the south of the country at the Liwa Oasis, moved to Abu Dhabi island. In Liwa, on the edge of the stark Empty Quarter, the Al Nahyan family lived a traditional Bedouin life, with animal husbandry and small-scale agriculture for their livelihood. Descendants of the Al Nahyan family, in alliance with other important Bedouin tribes in the region, have ruled the emirate of Abu Dhabi ever since.

The Trucial States

By the 1800s, the town had developed considerably, supported by the income from pearling, which brought in important trade and revenue. From 1855 to 1909, under the reign of Sheikh Zayed bin Mohammed (also known as 'Zayed the Great'), Abu Dhabi rose in prominence to become the most powerful emirate along the western coast of the Arabian Peninsula. His influence was profound and it was during his rule, in 1897, that Abu Dhabi and the emirates to the north accepted the protection of Britain. The British regarded the Gulf region as an important communication

Traditional fishing

link with their empire in India and wanted to prevent other world powers, in particular France and Russia, from extending their influence in the region. The area became known as the Trucial States (or Trucial Coast), a name that remained until the United Arab Emirates was born in 1971.

Independence

The British announced their withdrawal from the region in 1968 and encouraged the separate states to consider uniting under one flag. The ruling sheikhs, in particular Sheikh Zayed bin Sultan Al Nahyan and the ruler of Dubai, realised that by joining forces they would have a stronger voice in both the wider Middle East region and globally. When negotiations began, the aim was to create a single state consisting of Bahrain, Qatar and the Trucial States, but the process collapsed when Bahrain and Qatar chose to go it alone. The Trucial States remained committed to forming an alliance and, in 1971, the federation of the United Arab Emirates was created.

Formation Of The UAE

The new state comprised the emirates of Abu Dhabi, Ajman, Dubai, Fujairah, Sharjah, Umm Al Quwain, in 1972, Ras Al Khaimah. The creation of the country hasn't been without its problems, primarily due to boundary disputes between the different emirates. At the end of Sheikh Zayed's first term as president, in 1976, he threatened to resign if the other rulers didn't settle the demarcation of their borders. The threat was an effective way of ensuring co-operation but, although more focus is now given to the importance of the federation as a whole, the degree of independence of the various emirates has, to date, not been fully determined. It is however, led by Abu Dhabi, whose wealth and sheer size make it the most powerful of all the emirates.

Sheikh Khalifa bin Zayed Al Nahyan, Sheikh Zayed's son, was elected as president by the Supreme Council after his father's death. Sheikh Khalifa has promised to preserve his father's legacy, ensuring the continued growth of the UAE in order to meet the needs of its people. Apart from being an oil expert and head of the Supreme Petroleum Council, Sheikh Khalifa is renowned for his love of traditional sports, and his efforts in preserving them in today's modern times.

> ### An Admired Ruler
>
> Sheikh Zayed bin Sultan Al Nahyan was revered by his peers and adored by the public. As UAE president for 33 years and Ruler of Abu Dhabi from 1966 to 2004, he was responsible for many major economic and social advances both in Abu Dhabi and throughout the country, and his vision laid the foundations for today's modern society.

The Discovery Of Oil

Zayed the Great's death led to a period of conflict and, as his descendants fought for the leadership, the emirate fell into decline. In the 1930s, the combination of a world recession and the creation of the cultured pearl industry in Japan resulted in the collapse of the Gulf pearl trade. Its major source of income removed, Abu Dhabi slid from its position as the richest emirate, to that of the poorest.

The accession of Sheikh Shakhbut bin Sultan brought a reasonable degree of stability along with the first inkling that oil might be the answer to the emirate's economic problems. In 1939, he granted concessions to a British company to search for oil, but the huge offshore reserves were not discovered until 1958, by an Anglo-French consortium. Exports began four years later, launching Abu Dhabi on its way to incredible wealth. Sheikh Shakhbut's rule, however, was considered rather idiosyncratic and in 1966 the British exerted their influence, assisting in him being replaced by his brother, Sheikh Zayed bin Sultan Al Nahyan, the then governor of the oasis town of Al Ain.

Culture

The UAE's culture is tolerant and welcoming, and visitors are sure to be charmed by the genuine friendliness of the people. Abu Dhabi is a melting pot of nationalities and cultures, all of which are embraced without losing the cultural and national identity of which the UAE's people are justifiably proud; a culture and heritage inextricably linked to its religion. Women face no discrimination and are able to drive and walk around the city unescorted, unlike in neighbouring Saudi Arabia.

The rapid economic development of the last 40 years has, in many ways, changed life in the UAE beyond recognition. However, despite rapid development and increased exposure to foreign influences, indigenous traditions and culture are alive and thriving. The people of Abu Dhabi enthusiastically

Al Ain Fort

promote cultural and sporting events that are representative of their past, such as falconry, camel racing and traditional dhow sailing. Arabic poetry, dances, songs and traditional art are encouraged, and weddings and celebrations are still colourful occasions with feasting and music. As a mark of pride in the culture and national identity, most locals wear traditional national dress. For men this is a dishdash(a) or khandura – a full length shirt-dress that is worn with a white or red checked head-dress (gutra) which is held in place with a black cord (agal). Women wear a black abaya – a long, loose black robe, and a sheyla – a headscarf. Some women also wear a thin black veil to cover their faces and older women sometimes wear a leather mask (burkha).

Food & Drink

Traditional Arabic coffee (kahwa) is served on many occasions and, if offered, it is gracious to accept because coffee plays a special role as a symbolic expression of welcome. Even the pot itself, with its characteristic shape and long spout, has come to depict Arabic hospitality. Freshly ground and flavoured with cardamom, Arabic coffee comes in tiny cups with no handles. The cup should be taken with the right hand. The server will stand by with the pot and fill the cups when empty. It's normal to take one or two then signal you have had enough by shaking the cup gently from side to side. Until you shake the cup, the server will continue topping it up.

Pork is not part of the Arabic menu and the consumption of it is taboo to a Muslim. Many restaurants don't serve it, though you should find it on the menu in some of the larger hotels and it is also available in some supermarkets.

Local Cuisine

Abu Dhabi's restaurant scene has a truly global flavour, with most of the world's major national cuisines represented, and many of the fast-food outlets too. Eating out is very popular, but people tend to go out late so restaurants are often quiet in the early evenings. Modern Arabic cuisine reflects a blend of Moroccan, Tunisian, Iranian and Egyptian cooking styles, but the term usually refers to Lebanese food. From pavement stands serving mouth-watering shawarma (lamb or chicken sliced from a spit) and falafel (mashed and fried chickpea balls) sandwiches to the more elaborate khouzi (whole roast lamb served on a bed of rice, mixed with nuts), it's all here.

Shisha

Smoking the traditional shisha (water pipe) is a popular and relaxing pastime enjoyed throughout the Middle East. Shisha pipes can be smoked with a variety of aromatic flavours, such as strawberry, grape or apple. The experience is unlike normal cigarette or cigar smoking since the tobacco and molasses are filtered through water. Despite rumours that smoking shisha outside will be banned in the UAE it remains hugely popular. See p.220 for some of the best spots.

Religion

Islam is the official religion in the UAE and is widely practised. The religion is based on five pillars (Faith, Prayer, Charity, Fasting and Pilgrimage) and Muslims are called upon to pray five times a day, with these times varying according to the position of the sun. It is worth keeping in mind that Islam is more than just a religion, it is the basis for a complete way of life that all Muslims adhere to. There are plenty of mosques dotted around the city and, while most people pray in them when possible, most offices and public buildings have rooms set aside for prayers. Also, it's not unusual to see people kneeling by the side of the road if they are not near a mosque. It is considered impolite to stare at people praying or to walk over prayer mats. The abundance of mosques does of course mean that the call to prayer can be heard five times a day from the loudspeakers of the many different minarets, and not always in sync. Friday is the Islamic holy day and pretty much everything is closed until mid-afternoon, in accordance with the state and Islamic law.

During the holy month of Ramadan, Muslims are obliged to fast during daylight hours. Non-Muslims should not eat, drink or smoke in public areas during the fasting hours. You should also dress more conservatively. At sunset, the fast is broken with the Iftar feast. All over the city, festive Ramadan tents are filled each evening with people of all nationalities and religions enjoying shisha and traditional Arabic mezze and sweets. In addition to the shisha cafes and restaurants around town, many hotels erect special Ramadan tents.

The timing of Ramadan is not fixed in terms of the western calendar, but each year it occurs approximately 11 days earlier than the previous year, with the start date depending on the sighting of the moon. Parks and shops open and close later (many are closed during the day), entertainment such as live music is stopped, and cinemas limit daytime screenings. Eid Al Fitr (Feast of the Breaking of the Fast) is a three-day celebration and holiday at the end of Ramadan, when the new moon is spotted. It is the year's main religious event, like Diwali for Hindus and Christmas for Christians.

National Dress

On the whole, UAE Nationals wear their traditional dress in public. For men this is the dishdash(a) or khandura – a white full length shirt dress, which is worn with a white or red checked headdress, known as a gutra. This is secured with a black cord (agal). Sheikhs and important businessmen may also wear a thin black or gold robe, or bisht, over their dishdasha at important events (equivalent to a dinner jacket).

Arabic coffee

In public, women wear the black abaya – a long, loose black robe that covers their normal clothes – plus a headscarf called the sheyla. They are often far from plain, with intricate embroidery and beadwork along the wrists and hemline; sheylas are also becoming more elaborate and a statement of individuality, particularly among the young.

The headwear varies with some women wearing a thin black veil covering their face and others, generally older women, wearing burkhas – a leather mask which covers the nose, brow and cheekbones. Underneath the abaya, the older women traditionally wear a long tunic over loose trousers (sirwall), often heavily embroidered and fitted at the wrists and ankles. Younger females are just as fashion conscious as in other countries and often wear designer labels underneath their abayas, with trendy accessories.

Modern Abu Dhabi

The future of the emirate promises to be spectacular, with new developments bringing museums of international renown and luxury hotels.

Abu Dhabi has undergone tremendous growth; however, compared to the Dubai of the late 1990s and early 2000s, the emirate grew at a snail's pace. That all changed with Sheikh Khalifa bin Zayed Al Nahyan's rule. By changing real estate laws and setting up free zones, foreign money started pouring in and driving a boom that lasted a good five years, bringing the luxurious Emirates Palace (p.68), the stunning transformation of Yas Island (p.122) and Saadiyat Island (see p.122), as well as huge residential construction projects on Reem Island.

By 2009, however, with the financial crisis galloping at full speed throughout the rest of the world, there was no way Abu Dhabi could remain completely untouched. Nevertheless, its oil wealth meant the capital could afford to ride out the storm and even extend Dubai a US $10 billion loan to fight off its own creditors. Still, progress on some of the most significant projects in Abu Dhabi slowed, and other projects have been scaled back, including the ultra-ambitious Masdar City (see p.115).

The worst, it seems, is now over and the International Monetary Fund (www.imf.org) predicted that the UAE's GDP will grow 1.3% in 2010 after a small shrinkage in 2009. Of course, Abu Dhabi is positioned to grow the most, especially with the risk of Dubai's debt proposals.

Boosting Abu Dhabi's infrastructure and manufacturing sector is central to the UAE's plans to wean its economy off oil. Economists also see such spending as a key to reviving growth after the global recession by creating jobs, lowering the costs of running businesses and attracting more foreign investment.

People & Economy

The National Human Resources Development and Employment Authority claims that the population of the UAE will hit 7.5 million by the end of 2010. Given global economic conditions, this marks an incredible increase on a figure which stood at 4.77 million at the end of 2008. Abu Dhabi's population lies at around 1.75 million.

Following the global economic crisis in 2009, it was forecast that the UAE would experience its first population decline in many years. A partial UAE census took place in April 2010, however it is likely that results will not be published until summer 2011 at the earliest. Experts estimated a decline of anywhere between 8% and 17% for Dubai, with Abu Dhabi suffering to a lesser extent, but signs of an early recovery appeared to have buoyed population figures.

The UAE is considered the second richest Arab country, after Qatar, on a per capita basis. The country has just under 10% of the world's proven oil reserves (most of it within Abu Dhabi emirate) and the fourth largest natural gas reserves.

Prior to the crash of 2008 to 2009, the UAE enjoyed the benefits of a thriving economy growing at a rate of over 7% a year. In 2008, the UAE economy was worth Dhs.535.6 billion, with Abu Dhabi contributing 57% and Dubai 32% of the GDP. Successful economic diversification means that the UAE's wealth is not solely reliant on oil revenue and, in 2007, over 64% of the GDP was generated by non-oil sectors.

Tourism

Abu Dhabi has long been viewed by the rest of the world as Dubai's slow and less popular younger sibling but, in recent years, the capital has set itself up to become a major tourist destination in its own right. The Abu Dhabi Tourism Authority (ADTA) was created in 2004 to develop plans to transform the city into a leading global tourism destination. The city is set for almost exponential growth, with the tourism industry alone expected to generate a massive Dhs.26 billion in investment opportunities in the next eight years. An ambitious target has been set for 2015 with the capital hoping to quadruple its number of visitors from the 2005 level of 825,000. With over 1.3 million tourists visiting Abu Dhabi in 2007, ADTA is well on its way to achieving its goal.

Despite the global downturn of 2009, Abu Dhabi experienced an 8% growth in its tourism sector. However, business tourism is the capital's main focus and its premier venue for conferences, the Abu Dhabi National Exhibition Centre, which opened in 2007 but is still being expanded, has greatly contributed to the number of business events held in town. However, the exhibition centre is far from just a

Stunning architecture

business destination. Recent concerts such as Tom Jones and Harry Connick Jr, as well as large public events like the Abu Dhabi International Book Fair and Bride Abu Dhabi, help keep the public involved.

New Developments

When you see the amount of new development taking place in Abu Dhabi, it is easy to understand why the city is estimating three million yearly visitors by 2015. Billions of dirhams are being invested, but what is most impressive is the amount of thought that has gone into each project to retain the local heritage and culture and protect the environment.

The next 10 to 15 years will bring a tourism transformation to the city that will inevitably benefit both visitors and residents alike. Abu Dhabi plans to be the cultural capital of the Arab world, and many of its key projects focus on art, design and architecture, rather than business and commerce.

2008 saw the renaming of the Western Region of the Abu Dhabi emirate, now officially known as Al Gharbia, as part of this countrywide redevelopment. Al Gharbia covers 60,000 square kilometres of some of the country's richest oil and gas reserves, and is also home to spectacular natural scenery, delicate ecosystems and traditional Bedouin culture. The challenge facing Abu Dhabi's Urban Planning Council is making the best use of the region's resources while preserving its unique identity and environment so that it continues to attract visitors.

To cope with the rapid expansion of Abu Dhabi, a state-of-the-art terminal is being constructed at Abu Dhabi

International Airport that will increase passenger capacity to 20 million per annum. The development includes a new runway (completed in 2008), air traffic control tower, cargo and catering facilities, utilities and related infrastructure.

The UAE's official carrier, Etihad Airways, began operations in 2003 and in a very short period has grown into one of the world's busiest airlines, having carried over 17 million guests to 57 destinations since its launch. Abu Dhabi is a global hub, and Etihad plans to execute its ambitious plans for growth alongside the growth of the emirate.

Several new hotels resorts are in the pipeline including Angsana Resort & Spa Eastern Mangroves, on the outskirts of Abu Dhabi, which will focus on environmental protection and eco-friendly relaxation and adventure, and the Banyan Tree Al Gurm Resort (www.algurmresort.com).

For those keen to hit the shops, the Central Market redevelopment, set just back from the Corniche, should elevate the emirate's retail scene with its series of traditionally styled souks, shopping areas, hotels and nightlife.

The Saadiyat Island development (p.122) should boost Abu Dhabi's cultural offerings; it will be home to the Sheikh Zayed National Museum, the Louvre Abu Dhabi and the Guggenheim, all three of which are slated to open in 2013. Until then, Saadiyat's neighbour, Yas Island, will continue to hog most of the spotlight with its brand new hotels, its annual Formula One Grand Prix and the splendours of Ferrari World, which hosted 2010's Ultimate Fighting Championship and, when it opens officially in October 2010, will be the world's largest indoor theme park.

Abu Dhabi Checklist

01 Sheikh Zayed Grand Mosque

Sheikh Zayed Grand Mosque is one of the largest mosques in the world, and certainly one of the most beautiful. Walk around on your own, or take a complimentary tour and learn about Islamic worship.

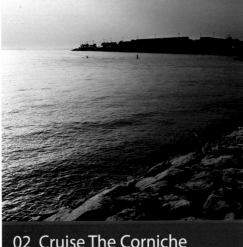

02 Cruise The Corniche

The Corniche has undergone massive reconstruction (some of which still continues) and is a popular spot; bikes can be rented for Dhs.20 for the day near the Hiltonia. For the best views that Abu Dhabi has to offer, a boat cruise along the Corniche (p.158) cannot be beaten.

03 Al Ain Oasis

This shaded, tranquil oasis contains many plantations, some of which are still working farms with ancient falaj irrigation systems. A peaceful and idyllic haven, the oasis is a great place for a stroll in the cooler months or to escape from the city.

04 Explore The Forts

Al Ain alone has 42 forts (more than any other Arabian city). Forts worth visiting in Al Ain include Al Jahili Fort (p.129), Hili Fort (in Buraimi) (p.128) and the ancient Muraijib Fort (Map 4 E8). In Abu Dhabi city, Al Maqtaa Fort (p.109) dates back 200 years.

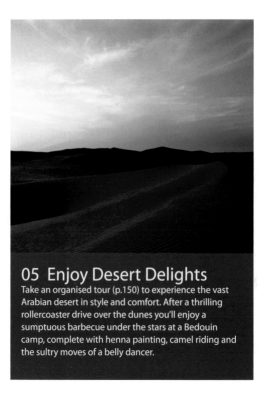

05 Enjoy Desert Delights

Take an organised tour (p.150) to experience the vast Arabian desert in style and comfort. After a thrilling rollercoaster drive over the dunes you'll enjoy a sumptuous barbecue under the stars at a Bedouin camp, complete with henna painting, camel riding and the sultry moves of a belly dancer.

06 Relax On A Desert Island

Located 250km from Abu Dhabi city, the desert islands are worth the road trip to enjoy the exclusive Desert Islands resort and get up close to nature at the Arabian Wildlife Park on Sir Bani Yas Island. The Al Gharbia Region is a definite up-and-comer on Abu Dhabi's tourism roll-call.

07 Get On A Camel

These 'ships of the desert' were once a key part of the Bedouin lifestyle, but today they are more likely to be giving rides on desert safaris (p.150). You can also watch camel racing (p.168), or browse the Al Ain Camel Market (p.191).

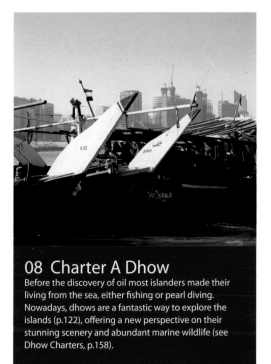

08 Charter A Dhow

Before the discovery of oil most islanders made their living from the sea, either fishing or pearl diving. Nowadays, dhows are a fantastic way to explore the islands (p.122), offering a new perspective on their stunning scenery and abundant marine wildlife (see Dhow Charters, p.158).

09 Shop Till You Drop

Whether you're looking for designer labels or just souvenirs, the many malls (p.196) and souks (p.190) are packed with ways to part with your hard-earned cash. Abu Dhabi Gold Souk (p.202), located in Madinat Zayed, is home to some of the largest gold shops in the Gulf, and the range of jewellery available is staggering.

Abu Dhabi Checklist

10 Try Life In The Fast Lane

Explore Yas Island (p.122), home to Yas Marina Circuit, which hosts the annual Abu Dhabi Grand Prix (p.59), the spectacular Yas Hotel (p.70) and Ferrari World theme park, which is set to open October 2010. With the best in shopping, leisure and residential areas to come, Yas Island is definitely the new hotspot.

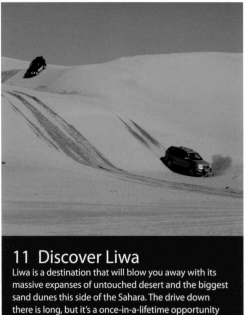

11 Discover Liwa

Liwa is a destination that will blow you away with its
massive expanses of untouched desert and the biggest
sand dunes this side of the Sahara. The drive down
there is long, but it's a once-in-a-lifetime opportunity
to experience unforgettable sunrises and adventurous
off-road driving.

12 The Heritage Village

The Heritage Village offers a glimpse into a way of life and culture that is far removed from the cosmopolitan and globalised city we see today. Test the effectiveness of a windtower, the earliest form of air conditioning, make friends with a camel, or brush up on traditional arts and crafts.

For Adrenaline Junkies

Away from the cities, the UAE has a lot to offer outdoor enthusiasts. For hardcore, experienced mountain bikers, there is a good range of terrain, from the super-technical rocky trails in areas like Shuwayah and Shawka, to mountain routes like Wadi Bih which climb to over a thousand metres and can be descended in minutes. Dubai-based company Hot Cog MTB (050 840 5901, www.hot-cog.com) is an active group who welcome new riders – they ride all over the country.

Dune and wadi bashing are among the most popular pastimes in the UAE. The desert, mountains and wadis offer stunning scenery and great challenges for experienced and novice drivers alike. Various tour companies offer courses where you can learn the art of manoeuvring a 4WD vehicle over sand dunes. Participants can usually drive their own car, or hire one (see Car Rental Agencies, p.62).

For Big Spenders

There is no shortage of places to shop in Abu Dhabi, whether you are after the international brands and designer stores in the malls or a more authentic Arabian experience in the souks. Abu Dhabi Mall (p.196) is the biggest of the bunch, with a vast selection of international stores. Local produce and traditional items can also be picked up at the souks. They are worth a visit for their bustling atmosphere, variety of goods, and the traditional way of doing business. If Abu Dhabi's selection of shops isn't enough, take the short trip over to Dubai to experience The Dubai Mall (www.thedubaimall.com), which is truly retail heaven.

Sheikh Zayed Grand Mosque

For Culture Buffs

One of the greatest cultural attractions in Abu Dhabi is the big, beautiful Sheikh Zayed Bin Sultan Al Nahyan Mosque (commonly known as the Grand Mosque) see p.110. The Abu Dhabi Cultural Foundation (www.adache.ae) has a new location in Sports City. It is home to the National Archives and the National Library. The foundation is a hive of activity with art classes, pottery and language classes held regularly throughout the week. If your visit to the region has given you a taste for local art, visit the Women's Handicraft Centre (p.141) just off Airport Road. Here you'll see women practising saddu (textile weaving, embroidering, basket weaving, palm frond weaving and tailoring); you can also pick up a camel bag and all manner or traditional craft items.

For Foodies

Dining on Arabic treats is a must while you are in town, whether you try one of the lively eateries such as Min Zaman (p.255) in Al Ain and Mawal (p.254) in The Hilton Abu Dhabi (www.hilton.com), or opt for the streetside stands selling shawarma (rolled pita bread filled with lamb or chicken carved from a rotating spit) and salad.

For Water Babies

There is plenty of fun to be had in the water, from diving (p.163) to watersports such as wakeboarding and waterskiing at the various beach clubs, such as Hiltonia (p.92). There are no waterparks in Abu Dhabi, but you can head over to Wild Wadi Waterpark or Aquaventure at the Atlantis hotel in Dubai.

For Architecture Admirers

The dramatic transformation of Abu Dhabi into a modern day metropolis brings with it a wealth of innovative architecture and design. The spectacular design of Yas Island (p.122), Capital Gate Tower (www.capitalgate.ae) and the circular Aldar HQ building near Al Raha have to be seen to be believed.

For Party People

The city has a reasonable number of nightclubs and numerous other venues that have schizophrenic personalities (bars or restaurants earlier in the evening, and later turning into a packed joint where you can cut loose on the dancefloor). Sip cocktails and show off your best moves at Cinnabar (02 681 1900) or enjoy R&B tunes at Colosseum (p.276).

City nightscapes

Visiting Abu Dhabi

The UAE warmly welcomes visitors and you can expect nothing less than exemplary hospitality, a growing infrastructure, and plenty to see.

Getting There

Abu Dhabi International Airport is undergoing a major expansion and redevelopment programme (see p.20), and Terminal 3, exclusively for Etihad flights, opened in 2009. The aircraft gates at the other terminals are arranged around a circular satellite, so you won't have to walk far to reach immigration and the baggage reclaim area. If you haven't arranged a hotel limousine pick up or hire car, a taxi to the city centre will cost about Dhs.65.

Completion of Abu Dhabi International Airport expansion is also expected to contribute to the boom in tourism. The project will upgrade the capacity of the airport to 40 million passengers a year. More than 40 airlines now operate out of the international airport with the key player being Abu Dhabi's national airline, Etihad Airways.

The airline first launched flights in 2003, greatly increasing the accessibility of the city to international travellers. It also offers free coach transfers from Dubai, thereby increasing its pasenger base significnatly. Etihad now flies to over 57 cities across six different continents and is adding, on average, one new route a month to its network.

Airport Transfer

There is a regular bus service between Abu Dhabi International Airport and Abu Dhabi city centre. The fully air-conditioned, green and white bus number 901 runs every 45 minutes, 24 hours a day, from outside the arrivals halls of Terminals 1 and 2. The fare is Dhs.3, however you will need to purchase an Ojra card (see p.61) and bus route maps are available from the airport. Call the airport on 02 575 7500 for more information.

Airlines		
Air France	800 23823	www.airfrance.ae
Air India Express	02 632 2300	www.airindiaexpress.in
Bahrain Air	02 633 4466	www.bahrainair.net
British Airways	800 0441 3322	www.britishairways.com
Emirates Airline	02 214 4444	www.emirates.com/ae
Etihad Airways	800 2277	www.etihadairways.com
flydubai	02 301 0800	www.flydubai.com
Gulf Air	02 651 6888	www.gulfair.com
Jazeera Airways	02 209 5555	www.jazeeraairways.com
KLM	02 403 8600	www.klm.com
Kuwait Airways	02 631 2230	www.kuwait-airways.com
Lufthansa	02 639 4640	www.lufthansa.com
Middle East Airlines	02 622 6300	www.mea.com
Nas Air	02 418 0820	www.flynas.com
Qatar Airways	02 621 0007	www.qatarairways.com/ae
Royal Jordanian	02 627 5084	www.rj.com
Saudi Airlines	02 635 1400	www.saudiairlines.com

Visas & Customs

Visa requirements for entering Abu Dhabi vary greatly between different nationalities, and regulations should always be checked before travelling, since details can change with little or no warning. GCC nationals (Bahrain, Kuwait, Qatar, Oman and Saudi Arabia) do not need a visa to enter Abu Dhabi. Citizens from many other countries (see Visas On Arrival, opposite) get an automatic visa upon arrival at the airport. The entry visa is valid for 30 days, although you can renew for a further 30 days at a cost of Dhs.620. All other nationalities can get a 30-day tourist visa sponsored by a local entity, such as a hotel or tour operator, before entry. The fee is Dhs.100, and the visa can be renewed for a further 30 days for Dhs.620.

Citizens of eastern European countries, countries that belonged to the former Soviet Union, China and South Africa can get a 30 day, non-renewable tourist visa sponsored by a local entity, such as a hotel or tour operator, before entry into the UAE. The fee is Dhs.100 for the visa and an additional Dhs.20 for delivery.

A special transit visa (up to 96 hours) may be obtained free of charge through certain airlines operating in the UAE.

Certain medications, including codeine, Temazepam and Prozac, are banned even though they are freely available in other countries. High-profile cases have highlighted the UAE's zero tolerance to drugs. Even a miniscule quantity in your possession could result in a lengthy jail term. Bags will be scanned to ensure you have no offending magazines or DVDs.

Visa On Arrival

Citizens of the following countries receive an automatic visa on arrival in Abu Dhabi: Andorra, Australia, Austria, Belgium, Brunei, Canada, Cyprus, Denmark, Finland, France, Germany, Greece, Hong Kong, Iceland, Ireland, Italy, Japan, Liechtenstein, Luxembourg, Malaysia, Malta, Monaco, Netherlands, New Zealand, Norway, Portugal, San Marino, Singapore, South Korea, Spain, Sweden, Switzerland, United Kingdom, United States of America and Vatican City.

Dos & Don'ts

The UAE is one of the most tolerant and liberal states in the region, but Abu Dhabi is rather more conservative than neighbouring Dubai. There still isn't much that you can't wear, but a healthy amount of respect for local customs doesn't go amiss, especially when shopping or sightseeing. Like most places in the world, the rural areas have a more conservative attitude than in the cities. Women should be aware that revealing clothing can attract unwanted attention, so very short skirts and strapless tops should be avoided. It is especially recommended that you dress more conservatively during Ramadan.

Lewd and drunken behaviour is not only disrespectful but can lead to arrest and detention. There is also zero tolerance to drinking and driving (p.43). It is courteous to ask permission before photographing people, particularly women. With prices for cigarettes low, smoking is very common. However, new laws have banned lighting up in malls and some restaurants so it's best to check the policy.

Essentials

Visiting Abu Dhabi

Local Knowledge

Abu Dhabi is an open-minded and hospitable emirate, where visitors from all over the world are made to feel both welcome and safe.

Climate

Abu Dhabi has a sub-tropical, arid climate and sunny blue skies and high temperatures can be expected most of the year. Rainfall is sporadic, falling mainly in winter (November to March). Rainfall averages 12cm per year in most of the emirate, but rain is more common in Al Ain due to its proximity to the Hajar mountains. Temperatures range from a low of around 13°C (50°F), on a winter's night, to a high of around 42°C (118°F), on a summer's day. The cooler months, November to April, are the most pleasant time to visit, when temperatures are around 24°C (75°F) during the day and 13°C (56°F) at night.

There are occasional sandstorms, when the wind whips the sand off the desert. This is not to be confused with a shamal, a north-westerly wind that comes off the Arabian Gulf and can cool temperatures down. Sandstorms cover everything left outside in gardens or balconies and can even blow inside, so make sure your windows and doors are shut fast.

Thick fog occasionally sets in on winter mornings, but is invariably burnt off by mid morning. The humidity can be a killer in the summer, making it feel far hotter than it actually is in July, August and September.

Crime & Safety

While the crime rate in Abu Dhabi is very low, a healthy degree of caution should still be exercised. It is unlikely that you will be the victim of a scam or a robbery, but it still pays to keep your wits about you. Keep your valuables and travel documents locked in your hotel safe, and when in crowds, be discreet with your money and don't carry large amounts of cash on you. Don't use an ATM if it looks like it may have been tampered with, and inform your bank. Money and gem related crimes run by con-men are on the increase, as are a whole variety of unbelievable scams, so don't be bullied into anything.

With a multitude of driving styles converging on Abu Dhabi's roads, navigating the streets either on foot or in a vehicle can be a challenge. Don't be too polite to tell your taxi driver to slow down if he is driving too aggressively, and if

Useful Numbers	
Abu Dhabi Municipality	800 555
Emergency	999
Abu Dhabi International Airport	02 505 5000
Al Ain International Airport	03 785 5555
Taxi	02 444 7787
	02 622 3300
UAE Country Code	00 971
Abu Dhabi Area Code	02
Al Ain Area Code	03
Directory Enquiries (du)	199
Directory Enquiries (Etisalat)	181

you are crossing the road on foot use designated pedestrian crossings (jaywalking is illegal), and make sure the cars are really going to stop before crossing. If you plan on driving yourself, make sure you know the rules of the road, exercise extreme caution, pay much more attention to your mirrors than you do normally, and be aware of what's happening around you at all times.

In An Emergency

Abu Dhabi is among the safest and most crime-free places in the world. Despite this, accidents and bad things do happen. The police are respected, involved in the community and very approachable. They are also easily recognisable in their ash grey uniforms. In an emergency, call 999.

If any valuables go missing, check with your hotel first, or if you've lost something in a taxi, call the firm's lost and found department. There are a lot of honest people in Abu Dhabi who will return found items. If you've had no luck, then call the Abu Dhabi Police to report the loss or theft; you'll be advised on the next steps to follow. Also make sure you keep a passport photocopy in a secure place to avoid hassle should you misplace it. If you do lose your passport, however, your next stop should be your embassy or consulate.

Electricity & Water

Electricity and water services in Abu Dhabi are excellent and power cuts or water shortages are practically unheard of. The electricity supply is 220/240 volts and 50 cycles. Sockets

Downtown Abu Dhabi

are mostly three pin of the British style, but some are two pin. The tap water is heavily purified and safe to drink, but most people prefer to drink locally bottled mineral water for the taste.

Female Visitors

Women should face few, if any, problems while travelling in the UAE. Women who are alone and who don't want extra attention should avoid wearing tight or revealing clothing and should steer clear of lower-end hotels and seedy nightclubs. No matter what, most women receive some unwanted stares at some time or another, particularly on the public beaches (periodically there is a crackdown on anyone suspected of harassing or staring at women on the beach). If you find yourself unable to escape an unwanted conversation, the mention of a husband (even a fictional one) should help you make a polite but firm getaway. The police are helpful and respectful – call them at any time if you face any unwanted attention.

It is perfectly acceptable to wear summery tops, skirts and shorts, especially in the more 'expat' areas. If you venture into more traditional or Arabic areas, it is best to dress modestly. In other parts of the country, people in small villages tend to be a lot more conservative.

Money

Most large shops, hotels and restaurants accept the major credit cards. Be sure to let your credit card company know that you will be travelling before you leave your home country. Otherwise they might freeze your account if they suspect fraud. Smaller retailers are sometimes less keen to accept credit cards and you may have to pay an extra 5% for processing. Conversely, paying in cash might mean a discount, so don't be afraid to use this as a bargaining chip. Cash is always your best option in the souks, unless buying expensive jewellery.

Money exchanges are available all over Abu Dhabi, they offer good service and reasonable exchange rates and are often better than the banks. Many hotels will also exchange money and travellers' cheques at the standard (poor) hotel rate. Be aware that exchanges tend to close between 13:00 and 16:30.

The monetary unit is the dirham (Dhs.) which is divided into 100 fils. Coin denominations are Dhs.1, 50 fils, 25 fils, 10 fils and 5 fils (although the latter two are very rare). Notes come in Dhs.5, 10, 20, 50, 100, 200, 500 and 1,000. The dirham has been tied to the US dollar since 1980 at a mid rate of $1 to Dhs.3.6725.

There is a huge network of local and international banks strictly controlled by the UAE Central Bank. Hours are Saturday – Wednesday, 08:00 to13:00 (some open 16:30 to 18:30) and Thursday, 08:00 to12:00.

All banks operate ATMs accepting a range of cards. For non-UAE based cards, the exchange rates used in the transaction are normally competitive and the process is faster and far less hassle than using traditional travellers' cheques. ATMs can be found in the airport, most shopping malls and hotels as well as most petrol stations.

Language

Arabic is the official national language, although English, Hindi,
Malayalam and Urdu are widely spoken. Arabic is the official
business language, but English is widely used and most road
signs, shop signs and restaurant menus are in both languages.
The further out of town you go, the more Arabic you will find,
both written and spoken, on street and shop signs. See the
table below for a quick list of useful Arabic phrases.

Basic Arabic

General

Yes	na'am
No	la
Please	min fadlak (m)/min fadliki (f)
Thank you	shukran
Praise be to God	al-hamdu l-illah
God willing	in shaa'a l-laah

Greetings

Greeting (peace be upon you)	as-salaamu alaykom
Greeting (in reply)	wa alaykom is salaam
Good morning	sabah il-khayr
Good morning (in reply)	sabah in-nuwr
Good evening	masa il-khayr
Good evening (in reply)	masa in-nuwr
Hello	marhaba
Hello (in reply)	marhabtayn
How are you?	kayf haalak (m)/kayf haalik (f)
Fine, thank you	zayn, shukran (m)/zayna, shukran (f)

Welcome	ahlan wa sahlan
Goodbye	ma is-salaama
Introduction	
My name is...	ismiy…
What is your name?	shuw ismak (m) / shuw ismik (f)
Where are you from?	min wayn inta (m) / min wayn (f)
Questions	
How many / much?	kam?
Where?	wayn?
When?	mataa?
Which?	ayy?
How?	kayf?
What?	shuw?
Why?	laysh?
And	wa
Numbers	
Zero	sifr
One	waahad
Two	ithnayn
Three	thalatha
Four	arba'a
Five	khamsa
Six	sitta
Seven	saba'a
Eight	thamaanya
Nine	tiss'a
Ten	ashara

Arabic isn't the easiest language to pick up, or to pronounce, but if you can throw in a couple of words of Arabic here and there they will usually be warmly received, at least with a smile. Most people will help you out with your pronunciation.

People With Disabilities

Most of Abu Dhabi's five-star hotels have wheelchair facilities but, in general, facilities for people with disabilities are limited, particularly at tourist attractions. Wheelchair ramps are often really nothing more than delivery ramps, hence the steep angles. When asking if a location has wheelchair access, make sure it really does – an escalator is considered wheelchair access to some. The Abu Dhabi International Airport is well equipped for physically challenged travellers and it is easily accessible. There is a special check-in gate with direct access from the carpark, as well as dedicated lifts, and a meet and assist service. Hotels with wheelchair accessible rooms include: Emirates Palace, Le Royal Meridien Abu Dhabi, Crowne Plaza, Crowne Plaza Yas Island, Hilton Abu Dhabi, Millennium Hotel, InterContinental Abu Dhabi, Shangri-La Hotel Qaryat Al Beri, and the InterContinental Al Ain.

Telephone & Internet

Etisalat and du are the local mobile telecoms companies and have reciprocal agreements with most countries for roaming services, allowing visitors to use their mobile in the UAE. Etisalat and du also offer useful prepaid services aimed at tourists. Visitors can purchase a SIM card and local number pre-loaded with calling credit so you can make local calls at the local rate. Both Etisalat and du SIM cards are available at most malls and mobile phone shops. Both of the local mobile telecoms offer short-term mobile lines for tourists. The lines can be picked up from one of the many Etisalat or du kiosks scattered throughout the big malls. The package includes a SIM card and usually a few minutes of calling credit that can be used for international calls or SMS. International calls from local mobile lines are much cheaper than hotel rates.

Time
Local time in Abu Dhabi is four hours ahead of UTC (Universal Co-ordinated Time, formerly GMT) with no summer saving time and so no clock changes. Thanks to the diversity of Abu Dhabi's residents and visitors, evenings are busy early on with families and late into the night with party-goers.

Tipping
Tipping practices are similar to most parts of the world. Service and luxury taxes are charged in hotel restaurants (which can add between 10% and 16% to the final bill). If you feel like rewarding good waiter service, then 10% is usual but give it to your waiter personally to be sure that it doesn't end up in the till. Tipping is common for petrol pump attendants, valet parkers and the guys who pack your shopping and take it to your car – Dhs.5 is the average. For hairdressers or beauty therapists, Dhs.5 to Dhs.15 should cover it. For taxi drivers it is regular practice to round the fare up to the nearest Dhs.5 or Dhs.10 as a tip, but this is not compulsory, so feel free to pay just the fare, especially if the standard of driving was poor.

Media & Further Reading

Newspapers & Magazines

There are several English language newspapers in Abu Dhabi. Abu Dhabi's first English-language newspaper, *The National*, was born in April 2008. It is a high-quality broadsheet with some top journalists from around the world. With its intelligent editorial and meaty lifestyle pieces, *The National* has quickly become one of the UAE's favourite reads. It costs Dhs.2 and there's also a good online version at www.thenational.ae. Other newspapers include the *Gulf News*, the *Khaleej Times* and *Gulf Today*, all of which cover local, regional and international news and lifestyle issues.

Many of the major glossy magazines are available in Abu Dhabi, but if they're imported from the US or Europe, you can expect to pay at least twice the normal cover price. Alternatively, you can pick up the Middle East versions of popular titles including *Harper's Bazaar*, *Grazia*, *OK!* and

More Info?

If you want to find out more about what's going on in Abu Dhabi, check out www.liveworkexplore.com for event listings or pick up a copy of *Live Work Explore* magazine. If you want to venture out of the city, pick up a copy of *Weekend Breaks Oman & the UAE* for the low-down on the region's best hotels. The *UAE Off-Road Explorer* is essential reading if you want to explore the country, and *UAE Road Atlas* will help you find your way back.

Hello! where you'll find all the regular gossip and news, with extras from around the region.

All international titles are examined by a censory board and anything offensive is crossed out with a big black marker. This is little more than an amusing inconvenience, and if you come across a publication that has been 'blacked out', it is an interesting souvenir to take home to show friends in more liberal countries.

Television

Most hotel rooms will have satellite or cable, broadcasting a mix of local and international channels. You'll find MTV, major news stations and some BBC programming, in addition to the standard hotel room information loop. The local television channels in Abu Dhabi generally leave a little bit to be desired but they often broadcast Arabic soap operas, talks shows and American sitcoms in addition to local news programmes.

Radio

The UAE has a number of commercial radio stations broadcasting in a range of languages, including Arabic, English, French, Hindi, Malayalam and Urdu. The daily schedules are listed in all local newspapers.

There are six English language music stations, all operating 24 hours a day. Emirates Radio 1 (100.5FM & 104.1FM) and 2 (99.3FM), Dubai 92 (92.0FM), Channel 4 (104.8FM), Virgin Radio (104.4FM) and The Coast (103.2FM) all play a mixture of old and new popular music, and have regular news broadcasts and traffic updates.

Public Holidays & Annual Events

Public Holidays

The Islamic calendar starts from the year 622 AD, the year of Prophet Muhammad's migration (Hijra) from Mecca to Al Madinah. Hence the Islamic year is called the Hijri year and dates are followed by AH (After Hijra). As some holidays are based on the sighting of the moon and are not fixed dates on the Hijri calendar, the dates of Islamic holidays are more often than not confirmed less than 24 hours in advance. Some non-religious holidays, however, are fixed according to the Gregorian calendar.

The main Muslim festivals are Eid Al Fitr (the festival of the breaking of the fast, which marks the end of Ramadan) and Eid Al Adha (the festival of the sacrifice, which marks the end of the pilgrimage to Mecca). Mawlid Al Nabee is the holiday celebrating the Prophet Muhammad's birthday, and Lailat Al Mi'raj celebrates the Prophet's ascension into heaven.

In general, public holidays are unlikely to disrupt a visit to Abu Dhabi except that shops may open a bit later.

Public Holidays

New Year's Day	Jan 1 (Fixed)
Prophet Muhammad's Birthday	Feb 26, 2011 (Moon)
Lailat Al Miraj	July 9, 2010 (Moon)
Accession Day	Aug 6 (Fixed)
Ramadan Begins	Aug 12, 2010 (Moon)
Eid Al Fitr	Sep 10, 2010 (Moon)
Eid Al Adha	Nov 17, 2010 (Moon)
UAE National Day	Dec 2 (Fixed)
Al Hijra (Islamic New Year)	Dec 7, 2010 (Moon)

During Ramadan however food and beverages cannot be consumed in public during the day and smoking is prohibited. These rules apply to Muslims and non-Muslims alike. Women should also dress more conservatively during this time. Food outlets and restaurants generally remain closed or offer takeaway purchases only during the day and then open up for Iftar in the evening.

Annual Events

Throughout the year the UAE hosts a number of major annual events which attract visitors from far and wide. The events listed below are some of the more popular fixtures on the social calendar and are well worth adding to your holiday itinerary.

Abu Dhabi Golf Championship   January

www.abudhabigolfchampionship.com
This is an established fixture on the European PGA Tour. The event has brought in some of golf's biggest names, such as Thomas Bjorn, Sergio Garcia, VJ Singh and Colin Montgomerie.

Al Ain Aerobatic Show   January

www.alainaerobaticshow.com
The Al Ain Air Show is a popular event (usually in January or February) held at the airport just outside Al Ain. The show has a festival atmosphere with tents and displays related to flying, aerobatics and stunt flying. Children are well catered for, with a play area filled with a variety of bouncy castles.

Dhow Racing

All year round

www.adimsc.ae

Scheduled dhow races take place throughout the year, mostly between September and April. The ones held off Abu Dhabi are short coastal races and the boats, many of which are old pearling vessels, have a shallow draught ideal for sailing closer to the Corniche.

Capitala World Tennis Championship

January

www.capitalawtc.com

Abu Dhabi's first major international tennis tournament was held in January 2009, and has become an annual event. Alongside the competition are other attractions for spectators, especially families, as well as a series of tennis-based activities and tournaments during the run-up to the event, including the Community Cup.

Powerboat Racing

March

www.adimsc.ae

The UAE is well established on the world championship powerboat racing circuit with Formula One (onshore) in Abu Dhabi and Class One (offshore) in Dubai and Fujairah. Abu Dhabi International Marine Sports Club hosts races from October to May including the final round of the F1 series.

Abu Dhabi Music & Arts Festival

March

Emirates Palace   www.admafestival.com

The successful Abu Dhabi Music & Arts Festival (ADMAF) aims to promote classical music and fine arts among Abu Dhabi

Al Ain Aerobatic Show

residents. In 2009, the festival featured the Bolshoi Ballet, Andrea Bocelli and Sir James Galway, among others, in 20 concerts spread over 13 days.

Red Bull Air Race   April
The Corniche   www.redbullairrace.com

Abu Dhabi is the traditional start for the Red Bull Air Race World Series. The Corniche is transformed into a unique racetrack with a specially built airport situated in the harbour. Spectators can view the action from the shore as the pilots race through the air just metres above the water.

WOMAD Abu Dhabi   April
The Corniche   www.womadabudhabi.ae

Peter Gabriel's World of Music and Dance festival is held in various locations across the world and made its first appearance on the Abu Dhabi calendar in 2009. Showcasing international music, dance and performing artists, the festival is free of charge and held on the Corniche, where visitors can also enjoy arts workshops and food from around the world.

Abu Dhabi Film Festival (formerly Middle East International Film Festival)   October
www.meiff.com

This festival had a stellar showing in 2009 and is arguably the region's premier film event. The film festival's cinema screenings and events include award-winning films from around the world. Along with the Dubai International Film

Festival, this is an important showcase for the growing regional film industry.

Abu Dhabi Desert Challenge   March
www.abudhabidesertchallenge.com
After the Grand Prix, this is the highest profile motorsport event in the country and is often the culmination of the cross-country rallying world cup. The event attracts some of the world's top rally drivers and bike riders who compete in the car, truck and motocross categories over four days. There are numerous checkpoints where the public can hang out to watch the daredevil participants scream past in their vehicles, which range from big monster trucks to simple quad bikes.

Etihad Airways Abu Dhabi Grand Prix   November
www.yasmarinacircuit.com
The brand new 5.6km circuit on Yas Island, located to the east of Abu Dhabi island, is a world-class, FIA sanctioned racetrack where race fans can enjoy a close view of the action. The track's first Grand Prix was a huge success and will continue to attract international fans for years to come.

Abu Dhabi Adventure Challenge   December
www.abudhabi-adventure.com
The Abu Dhabi Adventure Challenge is a multi-sport endurance race that sees teams of four people racing over six consecutive days. The disciplines are: sea kayaking, camel hiking, cross-orienteering, mountain biking, adventure running, rope climbing, and inline skating.

Getting Around

Abu Dhabi is compact, well laid out and easy to navigate. While public transport is limited, there are more than enough alternatives.

A car is the most popular and practical method of getting around Abu Dhabi. There is a reasonable public bus service (which on some routes is free), but walking and cycling are limited due to the searing summer heat, and there are no trains or trams.

Abu Dhabi's road network is excellent, and most main roads have at least three lanes. Streets are generally well-signposted with bilingual blue or green signs indicating the main areas or roads in and out of the city.

Visitors should find Abu Dhabi's streets relatively easy to negotiate. People often rely on landmarks to give directions; there is an official street name and numbering system, but people often refer to streets by their colloquial name.

The island's roads are built on a New York-style grid system and Abu Dhabi city is linked to the mainland by just two bridges: Al Maqtaa Bridge and Mussafah Bridge. The island is divided by Airport Road (2nd Street) which runs from the Corniche to Al Maqtaa Bridge.

In comparison to Abu Dhabi, Al Ain has developed in a less-organised manner but is nevertheless based on a rough grid system. The city is fairly spread out, consisting of about 10 major roads. Roundabouts are important landmarks for giving directions (such as the Clock Tower Roundabout in the centre of town).

Bus

The Abu Dhabi Department of Transport responded to the increasing need for public transport services by launching a two year bus initiative in 2008 with 258 new vehicles servicing the city and the suburbs. More buses have since joined the service and by the end of 2010, the Transport Department plan to have 1,360 buses on the road. With bus routes all over the emirate, as well as in the city, the service runs more or less around the clock and fares are inexpensive and cost as little as Dhs.1 for travel within the capital.

'Ojra' bus passes can be purchased directly at the bus stands or at any Red Crescent kiosk on the island (see www.ojra.ae for locations) in the form of one trip, daily or monthly passes. For more information on Ojra call 800 55555. Comprehensive bus route maps can be easily downloaded in PDF format from the bus page on www.abudhabi.ae.

The main bus station in Abu Dhabi is on Hazza bin Zayed Road and there are bus stops in many of the main residential districts. Since the end of 2009, there have been an increasing number of new bus shelters, some of which are air-conditioned, installed around the city to make waiting more comfortable. The Abu Dhabi-Dubai bus, Emirates Express, is operated jointly by the Abu Dhabi and Dubai municipalities. The 150km route takes around two hours and operates every 40 minutes between 06:30 and 21:30 from the Al Wahda Mall Bus Stop in Abu Dhabi. Return buses leave Dubai's Al

Ghubaibah station between 06:00 until 21:00. The cost per person has recently increased to Dhs.20 for a one way ticket. Abu Dhabi's transport department does not currently run a service between Abu Dhabi and Al Ain however Al Ghazal Transport does and you can contact them on 02 443 0309.

Driving & Car Hire

Over the past decades, Abu Dhabi has built (and is still building) an impressive network of roads; as a consequence, be prepared to come across lots of roadworks. While the infrastructure is superb, the general standard of driving is not. Drivers often seem completely unaware of other cars on the road and the usual follies of driving too fast, too close, swerving, pulling out suddenly, lane hopping or drifting, happen far too regularly. A good tip is to expect the unexpected and use your mirrors and indicators. There are

Car Rental Agencies

Avis	Abu Dhabi	02 575 7180
	Al Ain	03 768 7262
Budget		02 633 4200
Diamond Lease		02 622 2028
Europcar	Abu Dhabi	02 626 1441
	Al Ain	03 721 0180
Hertz		02 672 0060
Thrifty	Abu Dhabi	02 575 7400
	Al Ain	03 754 5711
United Car Rentals		02 642 2203

initiatives in place to help improve the situation on the roads, such as a ban on using handheld mobile phones, but many drivers seem to have stuck with their old, bad habits.

Driving is on the right hand side, wearing seatbelts is mandatory in the front seats, and speed limits are usually around 60 kilometres to 80 kilometres per hour in town, and 100 kilometres to 120 kilometres on major roads.

You will find all the major car rental companies in Abu Dhabi, plus a few local ones, and it is best to shop around as rates can vary considerably. Still, it's worth remembering that the larger, more reputable firms generally have more reliable vehicles and a greater capacity to help in an emergency.

Taxi

Taxis are reasonably priced, plentiful and by far the most common method of getting around. The more upmarket Al Ghazal or NTC taxis can be booked by phone (by dialling 02 444 7787 or 02 622 3300), but individually

Further Out

If you want to explore the UAE during your stay then you'll need a driver or rental car. The East Coast (p.144) is known for its wonderful coastline and watersports, all easily accessible in around a three hour drive. There is also a bus service to Dubai which runs hourly from Hazza Bin Zayed bus terminal. The journey takes two hours and costs Dhs.20. Contact the RTA on 800 9090 for more info.

registered taxis can be flagged down at the roadside. If you're struggling to flag a cab you're best bet is to get to a Mall, a main Hotel or the airport as this is where they tend to hang out in groups. All taxi companies service the airport and there are also specially registered airport taxis; the journey into town costs Dhs.70 to Dhs.80.

Most taxis are metered but some drivers will try to negotiate their fare with you. Keep in mind that this is totally illegal and you should insist on them using the meter.

Taxi driver's English skills vary and infuriatingly they often are not familiar with street names or places so it really helps to know where you are going and if you're new to the city, it's a good idea to take the phone number of your destination and a pocket map in case you get lost. If all else fails, if you are in an official taxi, the driver will call the control room to get directions.

The street taxis (which are being phased out) are easily recognised by their white and gold livery and by the green taxi sign on the roof, or by their silver livery and yellow sign on the roof (these are the new taxis). Daytime (06:00 to 22:00) metered fares in the city start at Dhs.3 and increase by an additional Dhs.1 for every subsequent kilometre of a journey. Most trips around the city shouldn't cost more than Dhs.15. Night-time fares are slightly more, with the starting fare at Dhs.3.60 and increasing by Dhs.1.20 per kilometre. The fare chart must be in plain view inside every taxi and whilst tips are welcome, it's illegal for a driver to demand one. If you have any problems with a taxi driver call 600 535 353. For more information visit www.transad.ae.

Get around on two wheels in the cooler months

Walking & Cycling

Cities in the UAE are generally very car orientated and not designed to encourage walking, especially as daytime temperatures in the summer months reach around 45°C. That said, the relative compactness of Abu Dhabi's main area makes walking a pleasant way of getting around in the cooler months, and an evening stroll along the Corniche is a must. Similarly, cycling is not common and therefore a little dangerous, although there is a safe cycle track at the Corniche.

Places To Stay

If it's opulence you're looking for then you've chosen the right destination. There are few places in the world that offer such jaw dropping luxury.

The standard of hotels in the emirate is so high that once you've spent a night or two in an Abu Dhabi five-star hotel you might find five-star hotels in other parts of the world a bit disappointing.

In 2010, Abu Dhabi Tourism Authority (ADTA) announced plans to introduce a new hotel classification system. As before, hotels will be rated from one star to five, but five star hotels will further be classified into silver, gold and platinum.

At present, good quality budget hotels are rare, but the selection of fantastic hotels and resorts might not be as expensive as you think. The initial price quoted, or the 'rack rate', is usually negotiable, and seasonal price fluctuations and special offers may make a stay in one of the palatial properties more affordable.

Most of Abu Dhabi's hotels are on the northern end of the island, near the Corniche, and within close proximity to the business district. The journey from the airport takes about 40 minutes and will cost around Dhs.70 by taxi. Many of the larger hotels have an airport shuttle service, which is often complimentary. Because restaurants and bars have to be part of a hotel or club to get a licence to serve alcohol, most hotels in the UAE are centres for social activity.

Al Ain Rotana Hotel
www.rotana.com
03 754 5111 **Map** 4 G8
This hotel location allows easy access to tourist attractions. The 100 rooms, suites and chalets are spacious and there is an outdoor pool and six dining and entertainment outlets.

Aloft Abu Dhabi
www.starwoodhotels.com
02 654 5000 **Map** 2 A2
Although located at the exhibition centre, Aloft is not a standard business hotel. It has a chic design which spreads to its restaurants, pool, gym and roof bar.

Crowne Plaza Yas Island
www.crowneplaza.com
02 656 3000 **Map** 1 H3
This recently opened hotel features 428 rooms, six bars and restaurants and an 25m outdoor pool. It also sits alongside the Links Championship Golf Course.

Desert Islands Resort & Spa
www.desertislands.anantara.com
02 801 5400
This luxurious resort features 64 rooms and full access to the Arabian Wildlife Park. A host of activities are on offer to guests, including 4WD safaris, hiking, snorkelling, mountain biking and kayaking.

Emirates Palace
www.emiratespalace.com
02 690 9000   **Map** 3 A2
This Abu Dhabi landmark boasts 392 opulent rooms and suites. There are 15 outstanding food outlets offering seven-star service. Guests can enjoy the 1.3km stretch of private beach and Anantara spa.

Fairmont Bab Al Bahr > *p.231*
www.fairmont.com/babalbahr
02 654 3333   **Map** 2 D1
The Fairmont Bab Al Bahr relies on minimalism and contemporary design to establish its own form of luxury. A private beach and several top restaurants round out an already impressive package.

InterContinental Abu Dhabi

www.ichotelsgroup.com

02 666 6888 **Map** 3 A3

This hotel offers 390 modern rooms and suites. There is a choice of superb eateries, a gym, outdoor pool, tennis courts and a private beach.

One To One Hotel – The Village

www.onetoonehotels.com

02 495 2000 **Map** 3 F6

The One To One offers a more personal experience than the big chains. It is close to the airport and it houses a number of good restaurants.

Qasr Al Sarab Desert Resort

www.qasralsarab.anantara.com

02 886 2088

This remote hotel is an extraordinary retreat with restaurants, a pool and spa along with its 140 rooms, 14 suites and 39 villas.

Shangri-La Hotel, Qaryat Al Beri

www.shangri-la.com

02 509 8888   **Map** 2 D2

The Shangri-La exudes luxury. The 214 rooms and suites all have private terraces with sea views. It offers a spa, two gyms, private beach and five swimming pools.

The Yas Hotel > p.IFC

www.theyashotel.com

02 656 0700   **Map** 1 H3

This futuristic hotel is an Abu Dhabi landmark. With 499 rooms and suites and over 1,600 square metres of conference space, it is one of the emirate's most recognisable hotels.

Park Rotana Abu Dhabi

www.rotana.com

02 657 3333   **Map** 2 C1

With views out over Sheikh Zayed Mosque, the Park Rotana is a modern and luxurious choice for business travellers. It has excellent business facilities, a spa and great selection of eateries.

Other Hotels

Tourist Club Area & Corniche East

The spectacular Abu Dhabi Corniche is the place to be; along with the Tourist Club Area next door, this area forms the main business district but also a key destination for tourism and leisure. Le Royal Meridien Abu Dhabi is home to Al Fanar: the city's only revolving restaurant, featuring panoramic views over the Corniche and the city's many skyscrapers, and offering delicious buffet dining; it also has 265 beautiful rooms and suites and 13 restaurants or bars in total (02 674 2020, www.starwoodhotels.com). The Crowne Plaza is just a few minutes' walk from the shopping district and beach, and offers stunning rooftop views (02 621 0000, www.crowneplaza.com), while the Beach Rotana Abu Dhabi offers some of the city's most popular dining outlets and direct access to the Abu Dhabi Mall (02 697 9000, www.rotana.com). With 12 restaurants, great leisure facilities and a private beach, the newly renovated Sheraton Abu Dhabi Hotel and Resort is always popular (02 677 3333, www.sheraton.com). Even the hotels that cater more specifically to business travellers are good options for tourists, thanks in part to their leisure facilities and restaurants. Good business hotels that double up as leisure destinations include Cristal Hotel (02 652 0000, www.cristalhotelsandresorts.com), Grand Continental Flamingo Hotel (02 626 2200, www.gcfhotel.net), and Millennium Hotel Abu Dhabi (02 614 6000, www.millenniumhotels.com).

CRISTAL SPA

Sanctuary in the heart of the city

Corniche West & Al Bateen

This is the neighbourhood of top hotels, attractive parks, a welcome sense of peace and a dash of heritage. One of the tallest, and most impressive, towers along this part of the Corniche is the Hilton Baynunah, which offers breathtaking views, a health club with indoor pool, and excellent business facilities (02 632 7777, www.baynunah.hilton.com). You'll also find the Hilton Abu Dhabi in this area, conveniently located between the financial district and Marina Mall. It has a private beach, swimming pools and a luxurious health club and spa, as well as some of Abu Dhabi's top nightlife destinations (02 681 1900, www.hilton.com). The Sheraton Khalidiya is in the upmarket Al Khalidiya area, and offers premium business facilities, a rooftop gym, a sundeck and pool (02 666 6220, www.sheraton.com).

Between The Bridges & ADNEC

Tucked between Massafah Bridge and Al Maqtaa Bridge, this area has become one of the capital's most prestigious, thanks in part to the beautiful Shangri-La Qaryat Al Beri Hotel (p.70) and it's many acclaimed restaurants and bars. It is also home to Souk Qaryat Al Beri, a lovely example of traditional architecture and home to a mix of local and international brands. Also here is the Traders Hotel (www.shangri-la.com) and the Fairmont Bab Al Bahr (p.68). At time of writing, the Grand Millennium Hotel & Spa Al Wahda was just weeks away from its official opening: with seven bars and restaurants, beautiful rooms and superb leisure facilities, it will further raise the profile of the area (www.millenniumhotels.com).

Top: Le Meridien Abu Dhabi; Bottom: Shangri-La Qaryat Al Beri

Yas Island & Off Abu Dhabi Island

Now fully on its way to becoming a unique tourism and leisure destination, Yas Island is attracting both crowds and big investment. The Yas Hotel (p.70) opened to coincide with the Formula 1 Etihad Airways Abu Dhabi Grand Prix (p.59), and there are other hotels already on this remarkable island. Centro Yas Island is the first offering from Rotana's new affordable-executive range: elegant interiors, large rooms and first-class amenities belie the affordable rates (02 656 4444, www.rotana.com). The Yas Island Rotana features gorgeous decor and superior service, as well as huge swimming pools, top-class restaurants and beautiful rooms (02 656 4000, www.rotana.com). Also on the island are the Park Inn Abu Dhabi, which is modern, colourful and suitable for those on a smaller budget (02 656 2222, www.abudhabi.rezidorparkinn.com), and the Radisson Blu Hotel (02 656 2000, www.radissonblu.com), which overlooks the Yas Marina Circuit and the Yas Links Abu Dhabi golf course. Not on the island but in the area is the Al Raha Beach Hotel, a boutique resort offering an escape from the city, where rooms feature sea views and the leisure facilities are superb (02 508 0555, www.danathotels.com).

Further Out

Away from the capital there is plenty to see in the emirate of Abu Dhabi, not least in Al Ain which is known as the 'garden city' due to its greenery. The InterContinental Al Ain Resort is set among landscaped gardens and offers a range of room options, family friendly facilities and seven food and beverage outlets (03 768 6686, www.intercontinental.com). The Hilton

GOLDEN TULIP
AL JAZIRA HOTEL & RESORT

Experience Fun Under the Sun

P.O.Box 26268 Abu Dhabi, UAE
T +971 2 5629100 F +971 2 5629035
info@goldentulipaljazira.com   www.goldentulipaljazira.com

Al Ain is a little closer to the city centre, but it still overlooks lush gardens; its restaurants and leisure facilities are popular with Al Ain residents (03 768 6666, www.hilton.com). Enjoying a lofty location on Jebel Hafeet, with beautiful views and clean mountain air, the Mercure Grand Jebel Hafeet has wonderful leisure facilities and a great pool play area for kids (03 783 8888, www.mercure.com).

The Golden Tulip Al Jazeera is located midway between Abu Dhabi and Dubai in remote surrounds. Accommodation is offered in the main hotel and in deluxe beach bungalows with dining options including Arabic-Turkish restaurant, Afandem (02 562 9100, www.goldentulipaljazira.com).

The Danat Resort Jebel Dhanna is about as far out as it gets: it is 240 kilometres west of the city, located right on the shallow waters of the Arabian Gulf with almost a kilometre of secluded beach. It is near one of Al Gharbia's (p.134) biggest attractions, Sir Bani Yas Island (p.134), and features leisure facilities that include watersports, tennis, a driving range and swimming pools (02 801 2222, www.danathotels.com).

Hotel Apartments & Hostels

The UAE is not an ideal budget traveller destination although Dubai, Sharjah and Fujairah all have youth hostels. For more information and exact locations visit www.uaeyha.com.

Another cheaper alternative to staying in a hotel is to rent furnished accommodation on a daily, weekly or monthly basis. Hotel apartments such as the Vision Hotel Apartments (www.visionhotel.net) usually come fully furnished and have a maid service, as well as a gym and swimming pool.

Come home to Vision Hotels

Travelling - whether for business or pleasure, for a short weekend or months at a time - can sometimes make you yearn for the comfort of your own home. At Vision Hotels, we understand that better than anyone else and that's why you are always our first priority. From more noticeable services such as free WiFi internet access all across the hotel and a state-of-the-art gym and spa to more subtle gestures like your personal iPod docking station, access to PS3 and Wii consoles, an extensive DVD collection and a warm smile whenever we see you, we go the extra mile to let you know that your comfort always comes first. *Come home to Vision Hotels.*

Exploring

Explore Abu Dhabi

Abu Dhabi offers activities, sights and excitement for all visitors without crowds. Enjoy the opulent luxury and fascinating heritage of this island city.

Between the calm green gardens, high-rise apartment blocks, elegant fountains, stunning corniche and luxury villas, is a truly vibrant city. Abu Dhabi is growing rapidly, and its evolution from quiet village to thriving metropolis has been remarkable, a testament to the vision of the late Sheikh Zayed, and the energy and drive of its people.

The high-rise central business district is home to imaginatively designed buildings which provide a dramatic backdrop to the corniche area. The Corniche itself is designed for play, with beautiful parks, walkways, cycle paths and picnic areas, all bordering the turquoise waters of the Arabian Gulf. Further inland the high-rises make way for beautiful villas, low-rise apartment blocks and quieter, tree-lined streets.

The following section gives an idea of what there is to see and do in Abu Dhabi, including museums, heritage sites, parks and beaches. If you're short of time, or want to explore further afield, an organised tour (p.150) is a great way to make the most of your visit. There's also a brief overview of what the other emirates have to offer. For more information, check out the *Abu Dhabi Explorer*.

Downtown Abu Dhabi

At A Glance

Heritage Sites

Museums & Art Galleries

Parks

Beaches & Beach Parks

Activities & Leisure

Sights & Attractions

Ras Al Akhdar & Breakwater

Ras Al Akhdar's pride is the iconic Emirates Palace. Nearby, Breakwater is home to a massive mall, a heritage village and some impressive views.

Ras Al Akhdar is the area at the north-western tip of Abu Dhabi island. It is dominated by the Emirates Palace Hotel (p.68), reputedly the most expensive hotel ever built. The classical architecture is complemented by state-of-the-art technology and the hotel houses a number of the capital's top restaurants (see Going Out, p.208). Bakarat Gallery (02 690 8950) is also located here and includes interesting exhibits of Islamic and international art. While Emirates Palace should be on every tourists 'must-see' list, you'll need a reservation before you can step inside.

The area's other attractions include the Abu Dhabi Ladies Club (p.88), which houses the luxurious Le Spa (02 666

Record Breakwater

One of the most famous landmarks on the Breakwater is the enormous flagpole next to the Heritage Village. For some time this was the tallest unsupported flagpole in the world (123m), until Jordan erected an even taller one (126m) in 2003. Jordan was then pipped by Ashbagad in Turkmenistan which raised its flag to 133m in 2008.

2228). There are also several open beaches in the area, which are quiet during the week but get very busy at weekends.

Breakwater is an area of reclaimed land connected by a causeway to the Corniche. The beachfront walkways are an extension of the Corniche development, and offer some spectacular views of the city. Marina Mall (p.202), one of the capital's largest, is also located here.

The fascinating Heritage Village (p.88) overlooks the Corniche. It is run by the Emirates Heritage Club and gives an interesting insight into the way that life used to be. You can test the effectiveness of the earliest form of air conditioning by standing under the windtower in the traditional houses made of barasti (dried palm leaves). There are loads of great photo opportunities, such as the chance to get up close and personal with an Arabian horse or a camel.

Once you've wandered around outside, head into the air-conditioned museum which houses a collection of artefacts including coffee pots, diving tools, Holy Qurans, jewellery, weapons and garments.

After visiting the village, sample some typical Arabic cuisine at the beachside restaurant (p.232). It has a great view of the Corniche, and it's close to a pleasant kids' play area.

Abu Dhabi International Marine Sports Club

02 681 5566

Breakwater

www.adimsc.ae

The Abu Dhabi International Marine Sports Club is the organising body for local and international powerboat events, traditional watersports and jetski races. The club has a marina with serviced berths, workshops and a showroom which stocks marine sports and fishing accessories. **Map** 3 B1

Abu Dhabi Ladies Club
02 666 2228
Al Ras Al Akhdar
www.adlc.ae

This excellent leisure club has a gym, pool, Jacuzzi, sauna and fitness studio, as well as a library, computers, arts and crafts classes, and the luxurious Le Spa. Non-members can buy weekly or fortnightly passes to access the club's facilities. **Map** 1A3

Heritage Village
02 681 4455
Breakwater

For an interesting glimpse into the country's past, a trip to the Heritage Village offers a chance to see what life was

People's Palace

Despite being one of Abu Dhabi's more exclusive venues, Emirates Palace hosts a number of events each year which are open to the public, including large-scale concerts in the gardens featuring international stars from Andrea Bocelli to The Killers. It is also the venue for some of the Abu Dhabi Film Festival screenings and events, and hosts performances from the Abu Dhabi Classics programme in its auditorium. Check www.liveworkexplore.com to find out about upcoming events.

Heritage Village

like in Abu Dhabi long before the discovery of oil and the subsequent development. Learn more about traditional crafts directly from local craftsmen who are happy to show you how it's done. It is a fantastic place to shop for souvenirs, like authentic pottery or exotic spices. Falconry displays are held on Thursday evenings during the summer months. It is open daily from 09:00 until 17:00 except Fridays when the hours are 16:00 to 21:00. **Map** 3 C1

If you only do one thing in...
Ras Al Akhdar & Breakwater

Take in the views of the city skyline from Breakwater.

Best for...

Sightseeing: Wander around the Heritage Village (p.88) at leisure and observe local men and women sharing their skills in traditional crafts.

Eating & Drinking: Enjoy authentic Arabic cuisine at a Breakwater restaurant, dine on views and sushi at Il Porto (p.248) or treat yourself to a traditional afternoon tea in Emirates Palace's Le Café (p.68).

Families: The Heritage Village (p.88) is the closest you'll get to travelling back in time, with its displays of Bedouin life.

Relaxation: Pick up picnic supplies at Marina Mall (p.202), then grab a spot on Ras Al Akhdar public beach before it gets too busy.

Shopping: Pay a whirlwind visit to Marina Mall's 250 shops and revolving restaurant.

Clockwise from top left: Marina Mall, exhibits in the Heritage Village, Emirates Palace

Corniche West

With two of the city's top hotels, a number of beautiful parks and an air of tranquility, this is one of the capital's most affluent areas.

In the west of the city, the Corniche begins at the end of the causeway to the Breakwater. Recently redeveloped, the Corniche is an attractive esplanade with pleasant parks and green areas dotted along it. The Hilton Abu Dhabi (www.hilton.com) stands on the land side while the Hiltonia Beach Club has pride of place on the sea side. The Hilton is one of the city's older hotels but is still one of its most luxurious. Its bars and restaurants are always busy, so if you're planning an evening out it's best to book ahead. The Hiltonia Beach Club (02 692 4205) welcomes day guests for a fee.

Al Bateen is a sought-after residential area, with a mix of low-rise apartment blocks and villas, along with great parks and a number of coffee shops. The Khalidiya Public Garden and the Khalidiyah Children's Garden (ladies and children only) are both well frequented by picnickers in the evenings and at weekends. Al Bateen is also home to the InterContinental Abu Dhabi (p.69), another of the city's well-established luxury hotels, which houses the highly-rated Fish Market and Chamas Brazilian Churrascaria (p.240) restaurants.

Further along the coast are the Bateen Wharf, Bateen jetty (with a number of marine supply stores around it) and the Bateen dhow yard. A visit to the dhow yard is essential, not just to absorb the evocative smells of freshly cut African and Indian teak, but also to watch craftsmen build magnificent dhows and racing vessels using age-old techniques. These wooden vessels can still be seen during dhow races off the Corniche or plying the trade routes around the Gulf and across the Indian Ocean. Al Bateen Wharf, the capital's oldest residential area, is being redeveloped and is still under construction. Parts of the area can, however, be explored, offering the chance to see some beautiful traditional architecture – most notably the heritage centre built by Abu Dhabi Heritage Club.

Bateen Dhow Yard
Al Bateen

The skilled craftsmen in this fascinating boat yard use traditional techniques to construct the dhows, which are still used for racing and for trade throughout the Gulf region and the Indian Ocean. Visit in the early evening and not only will you be able to get some wonderful photos of the sun setting behind the hulls, you may also be able to talk to the craftsmen – if they are not too busy they are usually happy to share an insight into their traditional craft. **Map** 3 A4

Khalidiyah Garden   02 666 1281

Taking up a whole block, this large park is popular with families. It has a variety of play areas, with equipment suitable for toddlers and older children. Its lovely grassy areas are great for lounging, with a number of large trees providing excellent shade. You can pick up picnic supplies at Abu Dhabi Cooperative Society on the south side of the park. **Map** 3 C3

If you only do one thing in...
Corniche West

Enjoy the seaside – relax on the beach, stroll the Corniche or chat to boat builders at the Dhow yard.

Best for...

Eating & Drinking: Head to Al Mawal (p.254) at the Hilton for a lively Lebanese meal with entertainment.

Families: Khalidiya Children's Garden is a ladies and children only park with rides and play equipment.

Relaxation: Meander along the Corniche or check yourself in for a leisurely day at Hiltonia Beach Club where you can enjoy swimming pools, a private beach and alfresco dining.

Shopping: Khalidiyah Mall (p.200) and Al Bateen Mall (02 666 1222) house a good variety of stores and entertainment for kids.

Sightseeing: Arrive at Bateen Dhow Yard before sunset and wander round chatting to the craftsmen. Get your camera out as the sun goes down for some great shots of the imposing hulls of the dhows.

Clockwise from top left: Al Bateen Marina, racing dhow, traditional architecture

Corniche East & Central Abu Dhabi

With the well-kept parks of the Corniche sandwiched between the clear blue waters of the gulf and the city's high-rises, this is an area of contrasts.

The redevelopment of Abu Dhabi's iconic corniche involved the reclaiming of a large strip of land and the creation of a number of new parks and attractions. The high-rise buildings which overlook it were once only separated from the sea by a six-lane road, but now a lush strip of greenery sits on the other side. An evening stroll along the Corniche should be part of every visit to the capital – this is where many of the city's residents come to meet, have picnics and relax, especially in the evenings and at weekends.

This area is generally seen as the city centre or main business district. Among the high-rises is the oldest building in the capital, the Qasr Al Hosn (the Old Fort, also known as the White Fort or Fort Palace), which dates back to 1793. It was the official residence of the rulers of Abu Dhabi for many years. The fort itself is not open to the public.

Sheikh Hamdan bin Mohammed Street (known as Hamdan Street) is a haven for avid shoppers, with local and international stores sharing the limelight with a number of independent restaurants and entertainment venues. At the end of Hamdan Street is the Marks & Spencer mall (Fotouh Al Khair Centre, p.199), which houses a number of international stores and a great cafe.

Further up Hamdan Street is the site of the old Central Souk. The area is currently under development as part of the revitalisation of downtown Abu Dhabi.

Gold is an excellent purchase while you are in the UAE, and you'll find plenty of it in the many jewellery shops lining the street before the Liwa Centre (p.200). So much gold is packed into the windows of these shops that at night the dazzling yellow glow spills out onto the pavements. The Hamdan Centre (p.190) is something of an institution and should be a stop on every visitor's tour. It is packed with small shops selling everything from souvenirs to (not entirely authentic) designer label clothes. It's also a great place to test your bargaining skills.

The Madinat Zayed Shopping Centre & Gold Centre (p.202) is where a number of the shops from the old Central Souk have relocated to. It is quieter than the other big malls, but comes to life in the evenings. There are some bigger shops here, but it is especially worth

Intrepid Explorers

While we like to think that we have covered every inch of Abu Dhabi, filtered out the missable and highlighted the unmissable, you may feel differently. So if you think we've left something out then we would love to hear your suggestions. Maybe it's an undiscovered heritage site or a fabulous restaurant that you want to shout about. Whatever it might be, you can log on to www.liveworkexplore.com and fill in our reader response form.

a visit for the smaller shops selling perfumes, clothes, fabric and haberdashery. The Gold Centre has some of the region's largest jewellery stores and is a great place to buy gold. If you want the classic souvenir of your name written in Arabic on a gold necklace, this is where to get it.

Some of the capital's top hotels are in this area, including Le Royal Meridien and the Sheraton Abu Dhabi Resort & Towers. While there are plenty of fine-dining restaurants within easy reach, don't miss out on the delicious authentic cuisine served at the many independent restaurants – good food at great prices, with a side order of atmosphere.

New Corniche

The Corniche should not be confused with the New Corniche (aka the Eastern Corniche), which runs along the eastern side of the island and is also known as the Eastern Ring Road. It too has had a facelift, and is a popular place for barbecues, picnics and a spot of fishing. The area near the Dolphin Fountains is the perfect spot for a family game of soccer or cricket.

Corniche Beach Park
Corniche Road

This two kilometre stretch of beach has excellent facilities including lifeguards, showers and toilets, and beach loungers and umbrellas for hire. There is a selection of coffee and fastfood outlets near the main entrance. The park is split with separate family and men's entrances, and there is space for everyone. Admission is Dhs.5 per person for families and Dhs.10 for single males.
Map 3 B2

Corniche Beach Park

Petroleum Exhibition

02 444 6900

Corniche Rd East, Al Markaziyah

www.adnec.ae

The revamped Petroleum Exhibition covers Abu Dhabi's phenomenal development. Spread across three rooms, there are scale models, photographs and documentaries (in English, French and German) and maps charting the earliest oil exploration in the desert and the Gulf, to the first oil export from Das Island in 1962. Entrance is free. **Map** 2 A2

Qasr Al Hosn

Cultural Foundation, Shk Zayed First Street

The Old Fort is the oldest building in Abu Dhabi, dating back to 1793. It was the official residence of the rulers of Abu Dhabi. The fort is part of the Cultural Foundation, and is currently under maintenance – although there are plans to reopen the fort as a museum and public monument. **Map** 3 E3

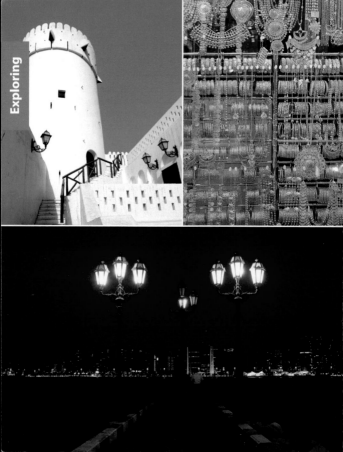

Exploring

If you only do one thing in...

Corniche East & Central Abu Dhabi

Tap into the heart of the city with an evening stroll along the Corniche.

Best for...

Eating & Drinking: Enjoy cheap chow at a pavement cafe, soaking up the atmosphere as the city starts winding down.

Families: Spend a day beside the seaside with sand castles and icecreams at Corniche Beach Park.

Relaxation: Take time out along the Corniche. In the evenings, it's a great place to mingle with residents enjoying a bit of leisure time.

Shopping: Haggle away at the Hamdan Centre (p.190) where you can engage in the traditional art of bargaining and pick up some amazing souvenirs.

Sightseeing: Head for the Gold Souk (p.202) – even if you're not buying, the sheer quantity of gold on offer is amazing.

Clockwise from top left: Qasr Al Hosn, Gold Souk, Abu Dhabi Corniche

Al Meena & Tourist Club Area

Amid bustling high rises, you'll find some of the city's best hotels and recreational facilities; it's no wonder that this is where fun-seekers gather.

Al Meena is the name given to the whole of the north-eastern tip of Abu Dhabi island, while the Tourist Club Area is an unofficial title given to the area from the Abu Dhabi Tourist Club to the Beach Rotana hotel and down to Al Salam Street.

Although the Tourist Club itself is currently closed for redevelopment, this bustling area is packed with high-rise apartment blocks, luxury hotels and some top shopping spots.

The Tourist Club Area's main draws are Abu Dhabi Mall (p.196), Abu Dhabi's second mega mall complete with multi-screen cinema and cafes, the Abu Dhabi Co-operative Society (p.196), for more chances to shop, and the Khalifa Centre (p.200), just behind the old Co-op, which is packed with souvenir shops.

Some of Abu Dhabi's top hotels are in this area. They are known for their great restaurants and bars, making the streets around them very popular in the evenings (for more information see Going Out, p.208). The Beach Rotana Abu Dhabi is linked to Abu Dhabi Mall – very handy if you're weighed down with shopping bags – and is home to the ever popular Trader Vic's (p.272) as well as many other great restaurants. The Culinary Village at Le Meridien, just down the road, also has a number of good restaurants – you can choose

Abu Dhabi Mall

between French, Indian or excellent Italian at Pappagallo (p.259), which has a picturesque terrace. For something a little lower key head to the bars and restaurants in and around Abu Dhabi Marina & Yacht Club (02 644 0300). This aging establishment is a little spit and sawdust but you're guaranteed a fun night out.

Abu Dhabi Airport City Terminal is across the road from the Beach Rotana hotel (www.rotana.com, 02 697 9000). Buses leave on a regular basis to Abu Dhabi International Airport, and most airlines have check in facilities here too.

Al Meena begins as an area of high-rises and ends at Port Zayed (a working port). Once you leave the high-rises behind, the area on the right is best known for the Carpet Souk (p.192). Most of what is sold is mass-produced but there are gems to be found if you know what you're looking for. The Club, one of the capital's most popular health and beach clubs, is also here but unfortunately is for members only.

To the left, past the Customs building, is Port Zayed. This working port is home to the Fish Souk (p.192) – the odours emanating from here can politely be described as 'colourful'. The adjacent Vegetable Souk is probably a more pleasantly fragrant way to experience the hustle and

Picture Perfect

Images of Abu Dhabi and the UAE, available in leading bookshops and supermarkets, captures the awe-inspiring wonders of the city, from the architectural marvels to the breathtaking landscapes. It's a perfect memento of your holiday.

bustle of a traditional market (p.192). Further on, you can browse through an impressive range of plants and household goods imported directly from Iran at the aptly named Iranian Souk. The Mina Centre, in the heart of the port, is a huge mall with a great bookshop (Jarir Bookstore), a supermarket and a children's amusement centre.

From Al Meena you can access the islands via the Sheikh Khalifa highway, an impressive stretch of tarmac that crosses picturesque mangroves before linking with the mainland beyond Yas Island. The highway is also the quickest route into downtown Abu Dhabi if you're visiting from out of the city.

The Club

02 673 1111

11 Street, Al Meena

www.theclub.com

An Abu Dhabi institution, The Club has been going nearly 50 years. This leisure facility is one of the most successful expat clubs in the capital, and guests must be signed in by a member. It has excellent facilities and it often puts on plays and concerts not found anywhere else in the city. **Map** 1 C2

The Dhow Harbour

The Dhow Harbour is particularly atmospheric at sunset when the fleet returns. The harbour is also the starting point for a number of dinner cruises, with the one run by the Al Dhafra seafood restaurant (p.233) being very popular – it sails along the Corniche every evening.

Even though there are some beautiful sights in the port, no photography is allowed in the area as Port Zayed is a working port with security restrictions in place. **Map** 1 C2

If you only do one thing in...
Al Meena & Tourist Club Area

Put your best bartering skills into practice at the souks.

Best for...

Eating & Drinking: Head to the Beach Rotana Abu Dhabi (02 697 9000, www.rotana.com) and enjoy a delicious buffet lunch at Rosebuds Restaurant & Terrace.

Families: Set sail from the Dhow Harbour for a tranquil dinner cruise organised by Al Dhafra Seafood Restaurant (p.233).

Shopping: Hit the retail jackpot with a trip around the 200 shops inside the Abu Dhabi Mall. With four storeys and around 26,000 visitors daily, this is an essential destination if you like shopping.

Sightseeing: Peruse the catch of the day at the Fish Market before browsing through the myriad of colours and shapes at the Vegetable Market. Select a rug at the nearby Carpet Souk and then head to the Dhow Harbour to soak up the atmosphere created by traditional wooden dhows and their exotic cargo.

Clockwise from top left: Beach Rotana Abu Dhabi, Carpet Souk

Al Safarat, Al Matar & Al Maqtaa

The southern end of the island boasts some of Abu Dhabi's most iconic landmarks. Here you can explore the emirate's heritage and look to its future.

This end of the island is currently undergoing major development, with several tourist, residential and commercial projects under way. Al Safarat is dominated by the Abu Dhabi National Exhibition Centre (ADNEC), a newly re-developed facility used for local and international events. The authorities have identified the conference and exhibition sector as a key priority for future development and ADNEC's state-of-the-art facilities attract a number of major international business events. It also hosts public events such as Summer In Abu Dhabi, a family sport, education and entertainment bonanza which runs in July and August. Visit www.liveworkexplore.com to find out what's on. Al Safarat is also home to a number of embassies and Zayed Sports City, which has a football stadium, ice rink and bowling alley. Access to the ice rink costs only Dhs.5 (plus Dhs.20 for skate hire); call 02 444 8458 for more info.

Old Airport Garden, near Zayed Sports City, is a lovely, established park with lots of shade and loads for kids to do. One side of the park is home to a few swings and small tidy gardens while the other side has an interesting ornamental display.

Al Matar, on the other side of Airport Road, is dominated by the Sheikh Khalifa Park. This is one of the city's newest parks and a major landmark. The gardens have an international flavour and are set amid canals, fountains, lakes and waterfalls – not really what you'd expect with the desert on the doorstep. There are play areas for children and picnic spots, making this a popular place to get some fresh air, play a spot of Frisbee or cricket in the open spaces or just relax with an ice cream and watch the world go by. Abu Dhabi is justifiably proud of its parks and this is one of the best.

Al Maqtaa is named after the heavily renovated Al Maqtaa Fort, which stands guard over the island. This area is dominated by the Sheikh Zayed bin Sultan Al Nahyan Mosque, known locally as the Grand Mosque, and the Armed Forces Officers Club & Hotel. The massive mosque, which holds up to 10,000 worshippers, is a major landmark and non-Muslims can visit it during set hours. The Armed Forces Officers Club & Hotel has some excellent recreational facilities, including two indoor shooting galleries and a good selection of restaurants.

Al Maqtaa Fort
Al Maqtaa

The 200 year-old, heavily renovated fort stands at the edge of the island and was built to fend off bandits. It is one of the few remaining of its kind in Abu Dhabi and, while you can't access the island on which it stands, it's a great photo opportunity and provides a wonderful contrast to the modern bridge. Map 1 E4

Sheikh Khalifa Park
Nr Al Bateen Airport, Al Matar

This landmark park has gardens set in a landscape of canals, fountains, lakes and waterfalls. Train tours of the park are available if you don't want to cover it on foot. It is home to kids' playgrounds, picnic facilities and an outdoor auditorium, and is popular in the evenings and at weekends. **Map** 2 C1

Sheikh Zayed Grand Mosque
Al Maqtaa

800 555

www.visitabudhabi.ae

A visit to this beautiful place of worship is a must as not only is it one of Abu Dhabi's most iconic buildings but it is also one of the few mosques open to non-Muslims. Public access is from Saturday to Thursday, between 09:00 and 12:00. Strict dress codes are in place so make sure you wear long, loose-fitting garments covering your wrists and ankles. Women must wear an abaya; these are provided free of charge at the mosque. Guided tours are available for groups of 30 or more and must be booked a week in advance. For group bookings and more information visit the website. **Map** 2 C2

Zayed Sports City
Al Safarat

02 444 8458

Zayed Sports City is a huge complex with a football stadium and an ice rink. The ice rink is one of the best places to go to beat the summer heat, but there are also a variety of other facilities including bumper cars, video games and a fast-food restaurant. **Map** 2 B2

Sheikh Zayed Grand Mosque

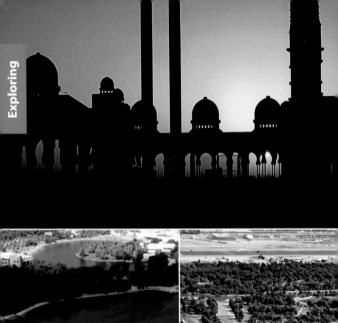

If you only do one thing in...
Al Safarat, Al Matar & Al Maqtaa

Learn about Islamic prayer rituals on the Sheikh Zayed Grand Mosque tour.

Best for...

Eating & Drinking: Enjoy a delicious lunch at the Armed Forces Officers Club & Hotel or at one of the area's independent street restaurants.

Families: Escape from the heat at Zayed Sports City, where you and the kids can enjoy a spot of ice skating, bumper cars, video games and fastfood.

Relaxation: Take a leisurely stroll or jump on the park train and tour Sheikh Khalifa Park enjoying the landscaped gardens and tranquil waterfalls. Head for the Maqtaa Bridge for some early evening sunset photos of the 200 year old Maqtaa Fort.

Sightseeing: The vast but elegant Sheikh Zayed Grand Mosque should be top of every tourist's 'must-see' list and makes a great photo opportunity.

Bain Al Jessrain & Al Raha Beach

Away from the city centre, mainland Abu Dhabi is home to newly developed areas and leisure facilities which are worth travelling further afield to explore.

The area on the mainland side of the creek is known as Between The Bridges (it sits between Massafah Bridge and Al Maqtaa Bridge) or Bain Al Jessrain. It is noted for large villas and compounds, but its focal point is the Qaryat Al Beri development (see map 2 D2). This complex is styled on traditional Arabic architecture and is home to a souk, the deluxe Shangri-La (p.70) and the neighbouring Traders Hotel (02 510 8888). Excellent leisure facilities lie within the Shangri-La including Bord Eau French restaurant (p.238), exclusive Pearls & Caviar (p.259), and CHI spa, while Traders is aimed more at business travellers. Running through the development are a series of waterways and canals on which Arabic gondolas or abras slowly meander through the unique architecture and lush gardens.

For more traditional architecture, across the road from the Qaryat Al Beri is an ornate Persian-influenced mosque. This small turquoise-blue structure is not open for tours but you can admire the craftsmanship from outside.

Next to the Traders Hotel is the new Fairmont Bab Al Bahr (p.68). The modern lines of this luxury five-star business hotel provide sharp contrast to the romantic architecture of Qaryat Al Beri. Among its attractions are Marco Pierre White

Steakhouse & Grill and a branch of Frankie's, Pierre White's joint venture with horse jockey Frankie Dettori. Nearby, Abu Dhabi Golf Club has some of the city's best golf facilities and a challenging 27 hole championship course.

Al Raha Beach lines the Dubai-Abu Dhabi highway on the approach to Abu Dhabi. The unmissable Aldar headquarters, shaped like a contact lens, towers over the area; on a clear day the reflections of the coastline in the building's mirrored face are quite impressive. The area is still under development but a handful of facilities are open to the public, including a shopping mall and Al Raha Beach Hotel.

Just beyond Al Raha and towards the airport is Al Ghazal Golf Club (p.160), a testing sand golf course which is home to the World Sand Golf Championship. Also near the airport is Abu Dhabi Falcon Hospital. Falconry is a national sport in the UAE and guided tours of the hospital can be booked in advance (02 575 5155). Visits can also be arranged to the Arabian Saluki Centre next door, where these impressive

Green Shoots

Near Al Raha Beach and the airport, Abu Dhabi's flagship green project, Masdar City, is taking shape. Eventually it will be one of the world's most sustainable cities, powered by renewable energy. The Masdar Institute of Science & Technology accepted its first students in 2009 at its temporary base at the ADNOC campus in Umm Al Nar. Find out more about the project at www.masdar.ae.

dogs, traditionally used in Arabia as hunting hounds, are bred
(www.arabiansaluki.ae).

Abu Dhabi Golf Club
Umm Al Nar Street

02 558 8990
www.adgolfclub.com

This club has excellent facilities including a par 72, 27 hole
championship course, a practice bunker, a driving range,
a short game area and a golf academy. The club hosts the
annual Abu Dhabi Golf Championship, a stop on the PGA
European Tour. Facilities are open to non-members on a 'pay
and play' basis. **Map** 1 F4

Al Raha Beach

Al Raha Beach Hotel and the Al Raha Mall are lively
destinations, particularly with Abu Dhabi residents who live
off the island. The hotel's eateries include Azur and Sevilla
restaurants, and day passes can be purchased for beach
access. Al Raha Mall has two cinemas and numerous shops,
restaurants and cafes. **Map** 1 G4

Souk Qaryat Al Beri > *p.195*

The centrepiece of the Qaryat Al Beri complex, the souk is
a modern take on a traditional Arabian market and is an
atmospheric place to spend time exploring. With regional and
international brands, it's a popular destination for shopping,
and the canalside alfresco dining options and coffee shops
make it a popular hangout for whiling away some downtime.
Left Bank (02 558 1680) is a great destination for sundowners
with a backdrop of impressive Grand Mosque views. **Map** 2 D1

EXPERIENCE THE DIFFERENCE

To make a booking or for more information,
call +9712 508 0555 or 800 ALRAHA

Al Raha Beach Hotel

If you only do one thing in...
Bain Al Jessrain &
Al Raha Beach

Treat yourself to upmarket trinkets at Souk Qaryat Al Beri.

Best for...

Eating & Drinking: Enjoy sophisticated sundowners at Left Bank (02 558 1680) or Pearls & Caviar (p.259).

Families: Spend a leisurely morning on Al Raha Beach Hotel's private stretch of sand and enjoy a poolside lunch under shady palm trees at La Piscine.

Relaxation: Opt for a round of golf at Abu Dhabi Golf Club's championship 27 hole course.

Shopping : Shop till you drop at Souk Qaryat Al Beri. Reward yourself with a pitstop at a waterside cafe in evocative surrounds.

Sightseeing: Capture the intricate facade of the Persian mosque on camera, then wander the souk to appreciate examples of traditional Arabic architecture.

Bain Al Jessrain & Al Raha Beach

Abu Dhabi Golf Club

The Islands

Many of Abu Dhabi's hidden treasures are just a short boat ride away, so take to the seas and explore the islands scattered along the coastline.

More than 200 islands pepper the coastal waters of Abu Dhabi and many of them are a stone's throw from the capital and can be easily accessed either by road or boat. The islands vary in size, and the majority are flat, sandy and uninhabited. The waters around the islands are rich in marine life, and you may be lucky enough to encounter humpbacked dolphins or endangered dugongs on your trip. Some of the larger islands, including the large man-made Lulu Island, are currently under development and are closed to the public.

Bahraini Island
40 minutes off the Abu Dhabi coast
You'll need to charter a private boat for the 40 minute journey to Bahraini Island but the journey is worth it to spend the day on its unspoiled beaches or at the wildlife sanctuary, and you may be able to spot dolphins en route. Tour companies such as Net Tours (02 679 4656) can tailor a day of island hopping for you.

Futaisi Island
5km south of Abu Dhabi Island   www.futaisi.com
Futaisi Island is famed for its wildlife, including turtles and some rare species, an authentic Arabian fort, a traditional

The Yas Hotel

mosque and mangrove lagoon. A boat service departs from
Al Bateen Marina at around 10:30 each day, returning in
late afternoon (02 666 6601). Overnight accommodation in
chalets is available.

Saadiyat Island

500m north of Abu Dhabi Island   www.saadiyat.ae

Saadiyat Island will eventually be home to Abu Dhabi's new
cultural centre which will include a Louvre gallery and a
Guggenheim museum, among other cultural venues. Most
of the island remains under construction but progress can be
viewed from the new highway which links it to Yas Island and
Al Meena. The first facility on the island to open is the Gary
Player-designed Saadiyat Beach Golf Club (www.sbgolfclub.
ae) which accepts day members. The newly inaugurated
visitor's centre showcases the plans for the island's future
development (www.saadiyat.ae). **Map** 1 D1

Yas Island

www.yasisland.ae

From groundbreaking in early 2007, Yas Island, a desert
island east of the Abu Dhabi city centre, was built up with
hotels, infrastructure and the brand new Yas Marina Circuit
just in time to host Abu Dhabi's first Formula 1 Grand Prix in
2009. The 5.6 kilometre track stands out for its unique design
which actually runs right through the island's flagship, The
Yas Hotel, giving about 250 very lucky VIPs envious views of
the proceedings from the bridge on race weekend. What's

more, the marina is incorporated into the circuit, so that the yachting crowd can not only make grand entrances but can view the race from their boats.

More modest F1 fans, however, can still enjoy some of the best views in all of Formula 1. This circuit brings the fans close to the action – each grandstand's location was chosen in order to supply the best views of any F1 venue.

In 2009, 50,000 people jammed the Yas Marina Circuit – including celebrities, dignitaries and hardcore fans – to witness as the UAE hosted its first F1 race. Racing is only part of the draw of Abu Dhabi's F1 weekend. The end of each racing day in 2009 brought performances from Jamiroquai, Beyoncé, Aerosmith and Kings of Leon to the outdoor arena at Ferrari World. Big names are set to headline again in 2010, when Abu Dhabi will again hold the final race of the Formula 1 season.

Development continues apace on Yas Island and the circuit will soon be just one of numerous attractions which will make Yas one of the UAE's premier tourist draws. One golf course has already opened its gates to players with another on the way, and Ferrari World (www.ferrariworldabudhabi.com) – the world's biggest indoor theme park, featuring the fastest rollercoaster on the planet amongst its 20 rides and attractions – opens in time for the 2010 Grand Prix, with a Warner Bros theme park to follow in the years to come. Several more hotels will join the seven already open on the island, as will a waterpark, several more marinas and the Yas Mall, where the largest IKEA in the UAE is already under construction. **Map** 1 H3

If you only do one thing in...
The Islands

Get up close with nature – there is fascinating flora and fauna to be discovered in the water and on dry land.

Best for...

Families: Stock up on supplies and charter a boat to Bahraini Island wildlife sanctuary where you can spot gazelle and Arabian oryx. Keep your eyes peeled for humpbacked dolphins in the waters as you pass by some of the archipelago's other islands.

Relaxation: Drive the Sheikh Khalifa Highway and survey the changing Abu Dhabi landscape. Check up on the progress of Abu Dhabi's island mega projects, admire the futuristic Yas Hotel and cross mangroves and coastal lagoons, taking in stunning views of unspoilt natural habitats.

Sightseeing: Catch the morning boat to Futaisi Island, where you can hire bikes or take a horseback or a minibus tour to explore the island's heritage sites including a renovated fort and a mosque. Explore untouched natural habitats and keep a look out for sea eagles, turtles and gazelles. Spend the afternoon relaxing on the beach.

Futaisi Island

Al Ain

The lush 'garden city' of the UAE lies in the shadow of the craggy Jebel Hafeet mountain and is surrounded by imposing red sand dunes.

Al Ain is the capital of the eastern region and Abu Dhabi emirate's second city. Its greenery and the fact that it is the birthplace and childhood home of Sheikh Zayed bin Sultan Al Nahyan, the former (and much-loved) ruler of the UAE, gives it special status in the hearts and minds of the people.

Today it only takes an hour and a half to drive from Abu Dhabi to Al Ain, but in the days before the discovery of oil, the journey took five days by camel. Most tour companies offer excursions to this fascinating city that straddles the border with the Sultanate of Oman; the UAE side is known as Al Ain and the Oman side as Buraimi.

The fortresses around the city, 18 in all, illustrate Al Ain's importance as part of the ancient trade route from Oman to the Arabian Gulf, and there is evidence of the area having been inhabited for at least the last 7,000 years. The city's archaeological legacy is of such significance that Al Ain is on the tentative list of Unesco World Heritage Sites.

Throughout his life, Sheikh Zayed pursued his vision of creating an oasis of greenery in the desert by initiating a series of 'greening' projects. As a result, Al Ain's seven natural oases are now surrounded by tree-lined streets and beautiful urban parks. The main Al Ain Oasis is home to palm plantations, many of which are working farms. The palms provide welcome shade and a haven from the noise and bustle of the city. Most of the farms still use the ancient falaj system of irrigation, which taps into underground water. If you do go exploring in the palm plantations, it is best to stick to the paved areas that weave between the walled-in farms. The Old Prison is also worth a visit simply for the stunning view of the surrounding town and oasis. The structure is a lone square turret in the centre of a gravel courtyard, surrounded by high walls. Unfortunately admittance is a bit hit and miss but if you visit as part of a tour you should be able to get in.

Al Ain's unique archaeological heritage and history is displayed at Al Ain Museum, on the edge of the main Al Ain Oasis. The museum has an interesting collection of photographs along with Bedouin jewellery, musical instruments, and a reconstruction of a traditional majlis. The archaeological section houses many of the finds from nearby Hili Gardens, and it's helpful to visit the museum before heading out to the gardens. The gift section houses an

Off-Road UAE

The UAE has some wonderfully contrasting landscapes that are well worth checking out, and the best way is by 4WD. If you're an outdoors type you should get your hands on the best-selling *UAE Off-Road Explorer*, which has 26 exciting off-road routes through desert, mountains and wadis, as well as info on places to see along the way.

unusual collection of items that Sheikh Zayed received during his lifetime, including golden swords and a golden palm tree.

Al Ain is home to the last camel market of its kind in the UAE, located within the Central Market. It's usually busy and the excited atmosphere builds as traders discuss the merits and value of each animal. The traders are generally very friendly to tourists and you'll be able to get some great pictures to take home with you, but remember to ask permission before clicking.

Buraimi is part of the Sultanate of Oman and you have to pass a border checkpoint to get there. The Buraimi Souk buzzes with local colour and atmosphere, and you'll find a few shops selling pottery, silver jewellery and woven carpets. The Al Hilli Fort, behind the souk, is a good starting point for exploring the Buraimi Oasis. The Al Khandaq Fort, located in the town of Hamasa in Buraimi, is thought to be around 400 years old. There are some amazing views to be had from the battlements.

Al Ain's biggest attraction, literally, is Jebel Hafeet. At 1,180 metres, the views from the top of this mountain are spectacular. If you are looking for a room with a view, the five-star Mercure Grand Hotel sits nearly at the top.

The Green Mubazzarah Park is at the foot of the mountain, and is home to hot springs, swimming pools and numerous chalets. It is extremely popular at weekends.

Al Ain Wildlife Park & Resort is the most progressive facility of its kind in the region and is home to over 4,000 animals, including apes, giraffes, crocodiles and a number of endangered species as part if its conservation programme.

Al Ain National Museum

03 764 1595

Al Muraba R/A

www.aam.gov.ae

This museum, on the edge of the main Al Ain Oasis, has exhibits on the archaeology of the area, the culture and heritage of the people, and a selection of gifts received by Sheikh Zayed during his lifetime. **Map** 4 G8

Al Ain Oasis

03 763 0155

Nr Al Ain Museum

The area is divided into palm plantations, many of which are working farms. Visit this cool, tranquil area to see the ancient falaj system of irrigation, which draws water from underground. Other oases include the Al Gattara Oasis which has a heritage village. **Map** 4 G8

Al Ain Wildlife Park & Resort

03 782 8188

Nr Jebel Hafeet

www.awpr.ae

Stretching over 900 hectares, this is one of the largest and best zoos in the Gulf region. As well as seeing large mammals, reptiles, birds and big cats, you can get up close to some rare and common local species such as the Arabian Oryx and sand gazelle. A park train regularly departs from the central concourse, providing a whirlwind tour of the zoo. Opening times vary throughout the year, so check the website. **Map** 4 G9

Al Jahili Fort

03 784 3996

Nr Public Garden

www.adach.ae

One of the largest forts in the UAE, the impressive Al Jahili Fort is over 100 years old and recently underwent extensive renovation. Now a cultural centre, it hosts large scale concerts as part of the Abu Dhabi Classics series as well as one off events and exhibitions. It is home to a permanent exhibition on British explorer, Wilfred Thesiger – known locally as Mubarak bin London – and his 1940s crossings of the Rub Al Khali (Empty Quarter) desert. Closed week days, open from 09:00 to 17:00 during the weekends. **Map** 4 G8

Jebel Hafeet

Rising abruptly from the surrounding countryside, Jebel Hafeet dominates the area and the views from the top are simply unmissable. On a clear day you can see the surrounding desert plains, oases, wadis and the Hajar Mountain range in the distance. The road to the top is in excellent condition with a number of strategic viewpoints along the way.

Central Market
Nr Town Centre

The Central Market takes the place of the old camel and livestock souks, but the camel market within it remains the last of its kind in the UAE. Conditions in the souk have improved dramatically with spacious pens for the animals, and while the general experience is more sanitised (and thus a little less characterful) than in the old souks, a visit to the market is a fantastic way to mingle with locals and experience trading as it has taken place for centuries. Hearing the excited owners discussing the virtues and values of their prize camels will give you a newfound respect for these ungainly (yet surprisingly expensive) animals. Open mornings only. **Map** 4 H9

Al Ain Wildlife Park & Resort

Green Mubazzarah
03 783 9555
Nr Jebel Hafeet

At the base of the imposing Jebel Hafeet mountain are the hot springs of Green Mubazzarah. They are a grand spot to rest and paddle in the supposedly curative waters. Chalets are available should you wish to stay overnight. **Map** 4 G9

Hili Archaeological Gardens
Mohammed Bin Khalifa St

The gardens are 10km outside Al Ain, on the road to Dubai. The area includes both an archaeological site and a public garden. There are remnants from a Bronze Age settlement (2500-2000BC), excavated and restored in 1995, and a number of the artefacts found are on display at the national museum.

If you only do one thing in...
Al Ain

Enjoy the lush greenery of the oasis.

Best for...

Eating & Drinking: Pop into the Mercure Grand Hotel for lunch on the terrace, or enjoy traditional Arabic food and entertainment in Min Zaman (p.255) at the Al Ain Rotana (p.67).

Families: Spend the day getting acquainted with creatures big and small at Al Ain Wildlife Park (p.129).

Relaxation: Enjoy a dreamy few moments surrounded by palm trees in the tranquil shade of the Al Ain Oasis. Watch the ancient falaj irrigation system in action at the palm plantations.

Shopping: Witness haggling at its very best at the Camel Market (p.191).

Sightseeing: Swot up on the city's unique archaeology and history in the Al Ain Museum. Drive up Jebel Hafeet to enjoy spectacular views from the 1,180m summit and dip your toes in the Green Mubazzarah hot springs on the way back down.

Clockwise from top left: Al Jahili Fort, Al Ain Oasis, Al Ain National Museum

Al Gharbia

With crystal clear seas and towering sand dunes, this undeveloped region to the west of the capital offers some of the UAE's most spectacular scenery.

Located to the west of Abu Dhabi, Al Gharbia makes up over two thirds of the UAE. Along its hundreds of kilometres of coastline can be found some stunning beaches, as well as a number of islands, which are increasingly being developed and promoted to visitors as high-end travel destinations. One of Al Gharbia's biggest attractions lies deep in the region's interior; Liwa is a mind-blowing destination with massive expanses of awesome desert and the biggest dunes this side of the Sahara. Whether you decide to rough it on a camping trip or stay in a luxury resort, you're guaranteed an unforgettable trip.

Desert Islands
Off Jebel Dhanna

The eight desert islands are located off the Abu Dhabi coast near Jebel Dhanna. They are serviced by a ferry from the jetty at Marsa Jebel Dhanna and by two weekly flights to Sir Bani Yas Island from Abu Dhabi. Sir Bani Yas Island was originally created as a private wildlife sanctuary by the late Sheikh Zayed. Now it is a luxurious island resort and home to the Arabian Wildlife Park's 160 species of animals which include cheetahs, hyenas, Arabian oryx and giraffe. The Anantara

Desert Islands Resort & Spa (p.68) provides a luxurious base from which you can go hiking, mountain biking, kayaking and get up close to the wildlife on a 4WD game safari. Alternatively, guests staying at the Danat Resort Jebel Dhanna can book a three-hour tour of the wildlife park.

Dalma Island has been inhabited for over 7,000 years and was once one of the most important centres of pearl fishing in the Gulf. Its history is captured in Dalma Museum and the various heritage buildings which have been restored on the island. The island is surprisingly verdant and can be visited via the ferry service from Marsa Jebel Dhanna on the mainland. The six Discovery Islands are still under development and closed to the public. Eventually they will provide luxurious eco-resort style accommodation along the lines of the Maldives.

Jebel Dhanna
230km west of Abu Dhabi

Located two hours west of Abu Dhabi, Jebel Dhanna is a great coastal getaway from Abu Dhabi. There are two hotels; the plush five-star resort Danat Resort Jebel Dhanna (www. danathotelgroup.com) and the lower rated Dhafra Beach Hotel (02 877 1600, www. ncth.com), both of which have beaches fronting on to

A Trip Of A Lifetime

To experience all that the incredible Al Gharbia region has to offer you'll need to leave civilisation behind and take on the desert wilderness. For help planning an unforgettable Liwa trip, check out the *UAE Off-Road Explorer* or contact a tour operator.

the shallow turquoise waters of the Arabian Gulf. Jebel Dhanna is also the departure point for Sir Bani Yas Island and Dalma Island – a new terminal called Marsa Jebel Dhanna will open shortly to ferry visitors by boat.

Liwa
225km south of Abu Dhabi city

Prepare yourself for the most adventurous off-road driving the UAE has to offer, and some of its most incredible scenery; a trip to Liwa on the edge of the Empty Quarter (or Rub Al Khali) is a must for any off-roader during their time in the Middle East. Stretching into Oman, Yemen and Saudi Arabia, the Empty Quarter is the biggest sand desert on the planet, and the sheer scale of the scenery and the size of the dunes, which rise to heights of over 300m, has to be seen to be believed.

The Liwa area is home one of the largest oases on the Arabian Peninsula which stretches over 150 kilometres and provides a surprising amount of greenery. While the main feature of Liwa is the desert, there are also several other attractions which are worth exploring along the way including tiny villages, a fish farm and some recently renovated forts. They are all interesting places to poke around in for an idea of the life that used to be in this remote corner of the country.

In order to access the biggest dunes and witness spectacular sunrises, camping is the most practical accommodation option. However, if home comforts are a necessity, the five-star Anantara Qasr Al Sarab (02 886 2088, http://qasralsarab.anantara.com) resort on the edge of Liwa has all you need to make your wilderness experience a little more civilised.

Off-roading in Liwa

Al Gharbia

If you only do one thing in...
Al Gharbia

Get out into the desert – whether on a tour company day trip or a long weekend camping, the sheer scale of the sand dunes have to be seen to be believed.

Best for...

Families: Combine a luxurious night at the five-star Anantara Desert Islands Resort with an exciting 4WD safari of the Arabian Wildlife Park, spotting giraffe, hyenas and cheetahs.

Relaxing: Take time out in the deliciously chilled lagoon pool at Qasr Al Sarab. Break your sun bathing with a spa treatment or a spot of archery.

Sightseeing: Take a few days to experience the full Al Gharbia landscape. Spend a day travelling the coast road and explore Ras Kumais at the tip of the final peninsula before the Saudi border, where you'll find excellent sea side camp spots, basic bungalows for hire, and crystal seas with great snorkelling and kayaking potential. Then head inland to tackle 300m tall sand dunes in Liwa, cross salt flats, explore the oasis and camp under the stars. Stop at the Emirates National Auto Museum on the way back to the city.

Top: desert retreat; Bottom: 'ships of the desert'

Off The Beaten Track

From traditional sports to mountain safaris, there are plenty of reasons to leave your sun lounger and discover the wonders of this diverse country.

Abu Dhabi Pottery
02 666 7079
www.abudhabipottery.com

Classes are available for both adults and children aged over five, giving you the chance to try hand building and the wheel technique. Classes cost Dhs.150 for adults and Dhs.85 for children, with supportive, knowledgeable instructors helping you create something original to take home. **Map** 3 C3

Al Maqam Camel Race Track
45km from Abu Dhabi, Al Ain Road

Despite their ungainly appearance, camels can reach surprisingly high speeds and a trip to watch them race is highly recommended if you're in town during racing season. Al Maqam is the closest racetrack to the capital and race meetings are held on Friday and Saturday mornings between October and March, from around 07:30.

Freediving UAE
050 613 0486
www.freedivinguae.com

Step away from the scuba gear and try diving in the way nature intended. Freediving UAE runs introductory and advanced AIDA courses, as well as regular training trips, so you can experience the incredible marine life of the Arabian

Gulf without the gear. Prices range from Dhs.1,200 to Dhs.2,780.

Noukhada Adventure Company   050 721 8928

http://noukhada.ae

The eastern side of Abu Dhabi island is flanked by a gorgeous mangrove forest which can only be explored by kayak, and eco-tour company Noukhada runs two-hour tours through the mangroves, focusing on the unique eco-system. Tours cost just Dhs.150 per person, including equipment rental.

Kids Park

www.kidsparkuae.com

The capital's first petting zoo, located outside the city on the Dubai road, the Kids Park is a five acre farm that offers children the chance to get up close to their favourite animals, including peacocks, ostriches, ibex, camels, horses, raccoons, ferrets, exotic fish and birds. The park is open every day and costs Dhs.20 per adult and Dhs.10 per child.

Women's Handicraft Centre   02 447 6645

Al Karamah Street

This government-supported centre consists of a series of huts in which local women practise traditional crafts, such as weaving, silver threading and henna body art. Perfect for picking up some traditional mementos but careful to photograph only the products and not the women. There's also a nice cafe on the premises, where you can sample traditional Arabic fare. Map 3 D5

Further Out

Beyond the capital, the UAE has spectacular sights and experiences, from bustling cities full of manmade wonders to mountain pools and desert retreats.

The six other emirates which make up the UAE lie to the north of Abu Dhabi and only occupy 13% of the country's landmass. Dubai, Sharjah, Ajman, Umm Al Quwain, and Ras Al Khaimah lie on the west coast, and Fujairah on the east coast. Each of the emirates has its own distinct character: Dubai is a glitzy tourist hotspot, Sharjah is the undisputed culture capital, and Fujairah is home to breathtakingly beautiful landscapes. If your stay in Abu Dhabi is long enough to permit exploration of the other emirates, you should definitely make the effort to experience their unique characteristics.

Dubai

Dubai is the place that the whole world is talking about. Although the breakneck speed of construction has slowed due to the global recession, it is still a fascinating city to visit. Among the high-rises you'll find the tallest building in the world, the Burj Khalifa (www.burjkhalifa.ae), a selection of the world's most luxurious hotels, some amazing leisure facilities (an indoor ski slope, with real snow, to name just one), designer hotels (including the exclusive Armani Hotel & Residences, www.armanihotels.com), celebrity-chef endorsed restaurants and several stunning beaches. There are also

a number of world renowned events worth checking out, including the Emirates Rugby Sevens in December, the Dubai Tennis Championship in February, The World Cup horse race in March and golf's Dubai Desert Classic (February) and Dubai World Championship (November).

Dubai's reputation as a progressive place is not undeserved, and it's a great destination for a night out whether you're after a slap up meal in a five-star hotel, sundowners at a casual beach bar or dancing till the early hours at an exclusive nightclub.

Renowned as the 'shopping capital of the Middle East', Dubai is the ultimate place for a shopaholic with a healthy credit limit. The enormous Ibn Battuta Mall, Mall of the Emirates (the one with the ski slope) and the record-breaking The Dubai Mall are all easily accessible from the highway.

Just be aware that the drive from Abu Dhabi can be pretty hair-raising. Defensive driving is not an option – it's a must.

East Coast

Even if you're only in the UAE for a short time, a trip to the East Coast is a must. You can get there in around three hours from Abu Dhabi.

The diving is considered better than that off the west coast, mainly because of increased visibility. Snoopy Island, off Dibba's coast, is a favourite spot for snorkelling. The East Coast is home to a few interesting spots, many of which are free to explore. The site of the oldest mosque in the UAE, Badiyah, is roughly half way down the East Coast, north of Khor Fakkan. The building is believed to date back to the middle of the 15th century and was restored in 2003. The village is considered one of the oldest settlements on the East Coast, and is thought to have been inhabited since 3000BC. Located at the northernmost point of the East Coast, Dibba is made up of three fishing villages, each coming under a different jurisdiction: Sharjah, Fujairah, and Oman. The villages share an attractive bay and excellent diving locations. The Hajar Mountains provide a wonderful backdrop to the public beaches. Further north, across the border into Oman, is Khasab, a great base for exploring the inlets and unspoilt waters of Musandam. You can stay at the Golden Tulip (+968 26 730 777, www.goldentulipkhasab.com), which can organise dhow cruises and dolphin watching, both of which are recommended, or the recently opened luxurious Six Senses Hideaway Zighy Bay (+968 26 735 555, www.sixsenses.com).

Further south on the coast lies Fujairah, the youngest of the seven emirates. Overlooking the atmospheric old town is a fort that is reportedly about 300 years old. The surrounding hillsides are dotted with more ancient forts and watchtowers, which add an air of mystery and charm. Abu Dhabi residents often use Fujairah as a base for exploring the rest of the coast. Hotels include Le Meridien Al Aqah (09 244 9000, www.starwoodhotels.com), and JAL Fujairah Hotel & Spa (09 244 9700, www.jalhotels.com).

Khor Kalba sits just south of Fujairah and is the most northerly mangrove forest in the world, and home to varieties of plant, marine and birdlife not found anywhere else in the UAE. A canoe tour by Desert Rangers (p.162) is the best way to reach the heart of the mangrove reserve.

Hatta

Hatta is a small town, nestled at the food of the Hajar Mountains, about 100km from Dubai city and 10km from the Dubai-Oman border. The road leading to Hatta from Dubai (E44) is a trip in itself. Watch as the sand gradually changes from beige to dark orange and then disappears, only to be replaced by jagged mountains. The famous Big Red sand dune lies off this road, and is a popular spot for dune driving in 4WDs or quad bikes. You'll also pass a row of carpet shops, ideal for putting your bargaining skills into practise.

Hatta is home to the oldest fort in Dubai emirate, which was built in 1790. You'll also see several watchtowers on the surrounding hills. The town itself has a sleepy, relaxed feel, and includes the Heritage Village (04 852 1374), which charts the area's 3,000 year history and includes a 200 year-old mosque and the fortress built by Sheikh Maktoum bin Hasher Al Maktoum in 1896, which is now used as a weaponry museum. The Hatta Fort Hotel (04 852 3211, www.jebelali-international.com) offers bungalow-style luxury rooms and sports and leisure facilities including shooting and mini-golf.

In the mountains beyond the village are the Hatta Pools, where you can see deep, strangely shaped canyons carved out by rushing floodwater. The trail towards the pools is graded, so a two-wheel drive car and some skilled driving should be enough to get you there. From the Dubai-Hatta road, take a right at the fort roundabout, then a left towards the Heritage Village, another left at the roundabout, and then the first main right. Drive through a second village; where the tarmac ends take the gravel track on your right. For tours see p.150.

Northern Emirates

North of Dubai are Sharjah, Ajman, Umm Al Quwain and Ras Al Khaimah. These emirates are smaller in size than Dubai and Abu Dhabi and are also less developed.

Ajman is the smallest of the emirates, but its proximity to Dubai and Sharjah has enabled it to grow considerably. It has one of the largest dhow building centres in the region, offering a chance to see these massive wooden boats being built with rudimentary tools using skills passed down through the generations. Ajman also has some great beaches and a pleasant corniche. Much of the nightlife revolves around the Ajman Kempinski Hotel & Resort (06 714 5555, www.ajmankempinski.com).

Umm Al Quwain has the smallest population and little has changed over the years. It is home to the expansive Dreamland Aqua Park (www.dreamlanduae.com). Two of the most interesting activities Umm Al Quwain has to offer are crab hunting and mangrove tours; the Flamingo Beach Resort (06 765 0000; www.flamingoresort.ae) offers both.

Ras Al Khaimah is the most northerly of the seven emirates but you can make the trip from Dubai in around an hour on the Emirates Road. With the jagged Hajar Mountains rising just behind the city, and the Arabian Gulf stretching out from the shore, RAK has some of the best scenery in the UAE. A creek divides the city into the old town and the newer Al Nakheel district. For a day trip, you should go the souk in the old town and the National Museum of Ras Al Khaimah (07 233 3411). From there you can explore the surrounding countryside and visit the ancient sites of Ghalilah and Shimal.

Sharjah

Before Dubai's rise to prominence as a trading and tourism hotspot, neighbouring Sharjah was one of the wealthiest towns in the region, with settlers earning their livelihood from fishing, pearling and trade. Sharjah is worth a visit for its various museums and great shopping. Its commitment to art, culture and preserving its traditional heritage is well known throughout the Arab world. Sharjah is built around Khalid Lagoon (popularly known as the creek), and the surrounding Buheirah Corniche is a popular spot for an evening stroll. From various points on the lagoon, small dhows can be hired to see the lights of the city from the water.

The Heritage Area (06 569 3999, www.sharjahtourism.ae) is a fascinating old walled city, home to numerous museums and the traditional Souk Al Arsah. The nearby Arts Area is a treat for art lovers with galleries and more museums. A must is Al Qasba (06 556 0777, www.qaq.ae), Sharjah's latest attraction, which has performance spaces and waterside restaurants. Another worthy stop-off is the Sharjah Natural History Museum (06 531 1411, www.sharjahtourism.ae).

Shoppers shouldn't miss the beautiful Central Souk, also known as the Blue Souk. The two buildings contain more than 600 shops selling gold and knick-knacks. This is one of the best places in the UAE to buy carpets.

Oman

Just a few hours from Abu Dhabi, you'll find the countless attractions of Oman. It's a peaceful and breathtaking country, with history, culture and spectacular scenery. The capital,

Musandam

Muscat, has enough attractions to keep you busy for a short break, including beautiful beaches, some great restaurants and cafes, and the mesmerising old souk at Mutrah. Out of the capital you will find many historic old towns and forts, and some of the most stunning mountain and wadi scenery in the region. Salalah, in the south, has the added bonus of being cool and wet in the summer. Isolated from the rest of the country, on the tip of the Arabian Peninsula, is the Omani enclave of Musandam. With its jagged mountains and fjord-like inlets, it has the moniker 'the Norway of the Middle East' and is a must-visit if you are in Abu Dhabi for any serious length of time.

A flight from Abu Dhabi to Muscat takes less than an hour and daily flights are operated by Etihad, Gulf Air, and Oman Air. There is also a bus service from Abu Dhabi to both Muscat and Salalah. For further information see the *Oman Mini Visitors' Guide*.

Tours & Sightseeing

Whether by boat, bus or 4WD an organised tour is a hassle-free way of maximising your sightseeing time and experiencing a different side to the UAE.

An organised tour can be a great way of discovering the Emirates, especially if you're only here for a short time. Whether you prefer activities, sightseeing or shopping, you'll find a tour to suit you. The majority of tours need to be booked in advance and most tour operators visit the main hotels in order to book tours for guests. Some trips may need to be arranged further in advance, especially if they involve travel to another emirate. Hotel concierges should have information on which tours are available and when and may even be able to get you a special deal.

Almost all tour operators offer the usual tours: city tours, desert safaris and mountain safaris. Some, however, offer more unique activities, such as fishing or diving trips, trips to see the Empty Quarter in Liwa, shopping tours and desert driving courses. Contact the companies on p.152 for some ideas. If they don't have exactly what you want, they're sure to know someone who does.

Big Bus Tours

Tour Abu Dhabi city on the top floor of a double decker bus, hopping on and off as you please and learning some fascinating facts en route. Find out more at www.bigbustours.com.

MICE facilities of Abu Dhabi Falcon Hospital the unique MICE venue in Abu Dhabi

Falcon World Tour Your Exclusive Tourist Destination Abu Dhabi Falcon Hospital

Star Media Advertising & Publishing

To make a booking
or for more information
call Mr. Amer Abu Aabed,
mobile 050-6660739
P.O.Box 45553, Abu Dhabi,
United Arab Emirates
Phone: +971-2-5755155
Fax: +971-2-5755001
Email: info@falconhospital.com
Web: www.falconhospital.com

ABU DHABI FALCON HOSPITAL

Tours & Sightseeing

Abu Dhabi Travel Bureau	02 622 1100	www.abudhabitravelbureau.com
Al Ain Golden Sands Camel Safaris	03 768 8006	www.alaings.com
Al Badeyah Eyes Tourism > p.153	02 556 6723	www.abet-uae.com
Al Mahboob Travel	03 751 5944	almahboob@eim.ae
Al Rostamani Travel	02 643 0500	http://alrostamanitravel.com
Advanced Travel & Tourism	02 634 7900	www.advancedtravels.net
Arabian Adventures	02 691 1711	www.arabian-adventures.com
Arabian Travel Express	03 766 6737	
Cyclone Travel & Tours	02 627 6275	www.cyclonetours.com
Desert Adventures	800 4230	www.desertadventures.com
Emirates Holidays	02 691 1722	www.emirates-holidays.com
Emirates Travel Express	03 765 0777	www.eteholidays.ae
Middle East Travel	03 764 1661	
Net Tours	02 679 4656	www.nettoursdubai.com
OffRoad Emirates	02 633 3232	www.offroademirates.com
Orient Tours	800 6789	www.orienttours.ae
Safar Travel & Tourism	02 418 0888	www.safar.ae
Salem Travel	02 621 1881	www.salemtravelagency.com
Sunshine Tours	02 444 9914	abusun@eim.ae

www.abet-uae.com

Half Day and
Overnight Desert Safari

A desert camp with calming and serene atmosphere yet full of fun for the whole family. Enjoy the once in a lifetime adventure and activities in the desert, significant to Arab culture and tradition of Bedouins.

Activities Included

▸ Pick up and Drop off
▸ Traditional Arabic Majilis
▸ Unlimited Soft drinks
▸ Barbeque Dinner Buffet
▸ Arabic Coffee and Date
▸ Sand Skiing
▸ Dune Bashing
▸ Sunset Watching
▸ Goat Ranch Visit
▸ Camel Riding
▸ Falcon Show
▸ Henna Tattoo
▸ Kids Play Area
▸ Quad Bikes for adults & kids

Al Badeyah Eyes Tourism

Al Raha Mall – First Floor, Phone: +971 2 556 6723, Fax: +971 2 556 6724
Mobile: +971 50 132 5848 ,+971 56 643 9434, Email: info@abet-uae.com
P.O. Box: 129633, Abu Dhabi - United Arab Emirates

Sports & Spas

Active Abu Dhabi

Best known as a sun-soaked luxury destination, Abu Dhabi offers much more – from golf and diving to a spot of relaxation at one of the spas.

Visitors to Abu Dhabi are sure to be delighted by the wide variety of sports and activities available, from the wonderfully indulgent to the adrenaline-fuelled. Winter (October to March) is the best time to enjoy outdoor activities (although many visitors take part in such pursuits all year round), whether it's mainstream sports like golf and tennis or alternative options such as caving, mountain biking, rock climbing and skydiving. For those less keen on the summer heat, there are plenty of indoor activities available, and most hotels have excellent gym facilities.

During the hotter months, early mornings and late evenings are the best options for outdoor activities, be it watersports, a round of floodlit golf, or a walk along the Corniche (p.96).

If you are interested in having a go at adventure activities such as climbing, off-roading, mountain biking, dune buggying or quad biking, then there are a number of reputable tour operators (see p.152) that offer tailored activity trips. Taking a trip out into the wilderness is a must, and there are various tours on offer (p.150). Places to see include the Rub Al Khali or 'Empty Quarter' (the last great frontier of uninhabited desert), the many oases

Mountain biking

hidden among the dunes or the dramatic wadis and jagged mountains rising out of the desert. If you've got the confidence (and the insurance) and are in a group you can hire a 4WD, pick up a copy of the *UAE Off-Road Explorer* and explore the unpaved expanses yourself.

Over the past few years, Abu Dhabi has made quite a name for itself on the international sporting scene. The Etihad Airways Abu Dhabi Grand Prix at Yas Marina Circuit (p.122) is now a fixture on the Formula One calendar, and the Abu Dhabi Golf Championship, which hosts several of the world's best golfers, is the curtain-raiser for the European PGA Tour. And after a successful hosting of the FIFA Club World Cup in 2009, Abu Dhabi will again host the event in December 2010.

Sports & Activities

Whether you're setting sail along the Corniche or teeing off on a world-class golf course, Abu Dhabi has much to offer the active visitor.

Dhow Charters

Al Dhafra
02 673 2266
Nr Fish Market, Al Meena
www.aldhafra.net

As well as dinner cruises, Al Dhafra has several traditional Arabic dhows available for charter. Most clients take their own equipment as there is only a limited amount on board. Food can be supplied at an additional cost. Charters cost from Dhs.150 per person for up to 8 people, or a dhow for 20 can be hired for Dhs.600 per hour. For more details on Al Dhafra, see the review on p.233 in Going Out. **Map** 3 H1

Blue Dolphin Company
02 666 9392
Al Khubeirah Complex
http://bluedolphin.dbansale.com

During this hour-long cruise, view the spectacular fountain, park areas and multi-coloured skyline of the impressive Corniche. The traditional Arabian dhow departs from the Breakwater every evening and then every hour, on the hour, for the rest of the evening. However, it is advisable to check sailing times with Blue Dolphin as occasionally the dhow is chartered for private parties. For more details call the number above or 050 492 6887. **Map** 3 A3

Shuja Yacht

02 674 2020

Le Royal Meridian
Abu Dhabi

www.leroyalmeridienabudhabi.com

Run by Le Royal Meridien, the Shuja Yacht offers dinner cruises that head along the Corniche for superb views of the Abu Dhabi skyline. The fare costs Dhs.221 per person, Sunday to Thursday and Dhs.225 for bunch at the weekends from 12:30 to 15:30. **Map** 3 F2

Golf

Abu Dhabi is rapidly making its mark as a leading international golf destination. Global television coverage of the Abu Dhabi Golf Championship, a European PGA tour event attracting some of the leading names in international golf, is dramatically raising the emirate's profile among the world's golf enthusiasts. There are already a number of options available for the keen golfer and the future looks even brighter, now several new championship standard courses are set to open, including two on Yas Island (one of which is open, but is for members only) and the Gary Player-designed Saadiyat Beach Golf Club (p.160).

Abu Dhabi Golf Club

02 558 8990

Sas Al Nakhl

www.adgolfclub.com

Located 30 minutes from the city centre, this is the venue for the Abu Dhabi Golf Championship. The club's facilities include the challenging 18 hole, 7,204 yard, par 72 National Course and the more forgiving 9 hole, 3,299 yard, par 36 Garden Course, plus a golf academy, a 350 metre driving range, practice facilities, a clubhouse, pro-shop, pool and spa. **Map** 1 F4

Abu Dhabi City Golf Club
02 445 9600
Saeed Bin Lahnoon St, Al Mushrif
www.adcitygolf.ae

This par 70 course boasts one of the longest par five holes in the Gulf, at 630 yards. Although there are only nine holes, there are alternate tees for the back nine. Green fees for visitors are Dhs.230 for 18 holes and Dhs.140 for nine holes, with cart hire costing Dhs.40 for 18 holes and Dhs.25 for nine holes. Range balls cost Dhs.10 per bucket for members and Dhs.20 for non-members. Competitions are held each Friday.
Map 1 C4

Al Ain Golf Club
03 768 6808
Nr InterContinental Al Ain Resort, Niyadat

The Al Ain Golf Club, east of the InterContinental Hotel, boasts an 18 hole sand course and a floodlit driving range. Handicaps gained here are valid internationally. Visitors are welcome, but should phone ahead. The sand is treated and compacted, creating a smooth surface that putts similar to a green. **Map** 4 H9

Al Ghazal Golf Club
02 575 8040
Nr Abu Dhabi Intl Airport
www.alghazalgolf.ae

This purpose-built 18 hole sand golf course, driving range, academy and licensed clubhouse is situated two minutes from the capital's airport, and has hosted the World Sand Golf Championship. Anyone can play here, including transit passengers with a few hours to kill – airlines can arrange free 96-hour passenger transit visas for travellers who want to play golf or use the facilities. **Map** 1 J4

Abu Dhabi Golf Club

Saadiyat Beach Golf Club

02 557 8000

Saadiyat Island

www.sbgolfclub.ae

The 72 Par, 18 hole course at Saadiyat Beach Golf Club was designed by Gary Player and should provide enough to challenge passionate golfers. For the less experienced, the Golf Institute by Troon Golf offers the chance to perfect your swing with an introduction to the golf course and a junior development programme. **Map** 1 D1

Hilton Al Ain Golf Club

03 768 6666

Hilton Al Ain

www.al-ain.hilton.com

The holes of this par three course average about 80 yards in length but, though short, can be tough to play. The course has nearly 30 bunkers and very small quick greens. It is open to non-members, and lessons are available. There is an entrance fee of Dhs.10 for non-members and green fees are Dhs.30; club hire starts from Dhs.30 for a half set. **Map** 4 H8

Wadi & Dune Bashing

Bouncing over the dunes in a buggy is exhilarating, addictive, and definitely one of the best ways to experience the desert. A popular location for dune buggies and quad bike riders is behind Al Ain airport, where locals and expats go to take advantage of the clean dunes and wide open spaces. Desert Rangers (04 357 2233, www.desertrangers.com), in Dubai, offer dune buggy tours, where you can enjoy all the thrills and spills of this extreme sport in the safest possible way – they provide training, all the safety equipment you'll need, and an experienced leader to guide you through the dunes. Alternatively, you can hire a quad bike from independent companies, most commonly found at the Big Red area on the road from Dubai to Hatta. A variety of quads are available on an hourly basis, although unlike dune buggies, quad bikes have no roll bar, so be very careful – accidents do happen.

Most car rental agencies offer visitors 4WDs capable of desert driving. If renting a 4WD, make sure you get the details of the insurance plan, as many rental insurers won't cover damage caused by off-roading. If you do venture out into the desert, it is a good idea to have at least one experienced driver and one other car to help tow you out if you get stuck. Most major tour companies offer a range of desert and mountain safaris if you'd rather leave the driving to the professionals.

Driving in wadis is usually a bit more straightforward. Wadis are (usually) dry gullies, carved through the rock by rushing floodwaters, following the course of seasonal rivers. When out in a wadi keep your eyes open for rare, but not impossible, thunder storms developing. The wadis can fill up quickly and you will need to make your way to higher ground pretty fast to avoid flash floods. For further information and tips on off-road driving in the UAE, check out the *UAE Off-Road Explorer*.

Watersports & Diving

With an ideal climate and the warm waters of the Gulf on its doorstep, Abu Dhabi is a great location for watersports. The Beach Rotana Abu Dhabi (p.72) in the Tourist Club area offers several options, including waterskiing, wakeboarding and windsurfing. Outside Abu Dhabi island, Al Raha Beach Hotel (p.76) rents jetskis. Most hotels contract out their watersports operations, so be sure the company you deal with has full insurance and that the equipment is in good order.

Kitesurfing has taken off in the emirate and there are several instructors with whom you can set up a two or three-hour lesson that includes equipment rental. For a listing of Abu Dhabi-based kitesurfing instructors, visit www.ad-kitesurfing.net.

The waters around the UAE are rich in a variety of marine and coral life as well as several submerged wrecks. In addition to exotic fish, such as clownfish and seahorses, you can see barracuda, spotted eagle rays, moray eels, small sharks, stingrays and sea turtles.

Most dive companies also organise trips to Musandam, the spectacular Omani enclave north of the UAE. For further information on diving in the UAE and Musandam, refer to the *UAE Underwater Explorer*, available at bookshops.

Snorkelling equipment is available for hire at most hotels or dive centres. Alternatively you can hire a car and take a trip to Snoopy Island near the Sandy Beach Hotel in Dibba (where you can hire snorkelling gear). Located on the UAE's east coast it is one of the best locations for snorkelling and diving.

Abu Dhabi Sub Aqua Club
02 673 1111
The Club, Al Meena   www.the-club.com

This club is affiliated to the British Sub Aqua Club (BSAC), so safety standards are high, and training courses are regularly held for all standards, including beginners. Dive trips are at weekends and include locations around Abu Dhabi, Musandam and Khor Fakkan on the east coast, where the club rents a villa. Membership is only open to members of The Club (p.105). For more information see the website. **Map** 1 C2

Arabian Divers & Sportfishing Charters > *p.165*
050 614 6931
Al Bateen Marina, Al Bateen   www.fishabudhabi.com

This divers' group has over 10 years' experience in diving and boat charters. It has a complete range of on-site facilities in the Al Bateen Marina, including a shop, a classroom, a training pool and boat charters. The club offers individual attention and small diving groups, making sure that safety comes first. PADI courses from beginner to advanced are available. **Map** 3 B5

Sandy Beach Diving Centre
09 244 5555/5354
Sandy Beach Hotel & Resort, Fujairah   www.sandybm.com

This dive centre offers a qualified team of instructors and support staff. Its famous house reef, Snoopy Island, is alive

with marine life and is excellent for snorkelling and diving. Trips to Dibba, Khor Fakkan and Musandam are also offered.

7 Seas Divers

Nr Khor Fakkan Souk, East Coast

09 238 7400
www.7seasdivers.com

This PADI dive centre offers day and night diving trips to sites around Khor Fakkan, Musandam and Lima Rock. Training is provided from beginner to instructor level, in a variety of languages.

Motorsports

The UAE deserts provide ideal locations for rallying, and many events are organised throughout the year by the Emirates Motor Sports Federation (EMSF). In 2009, Abu Dhabi hosted its first ever Formula 1 World Championship, held at the new Yas Island Marina Circuit. The Formula 1 Etihad Airways Abu Dhabi Grand Prix (p.59) was a high-profile three-day event which included concert performances from top acts including Beyoncé, Aerosmith and Kings of Leon. The Grand Prix is set to be held again towards the end of 2010.

The annual Abu Dhabi Desert Challenge, held in March, is a great spectator event for rally fans (www.uaedesertchallenge. com). Other events throughout the year include the Spring Desert Rally (4WD), Peace Rally (saloons); Jeep Jamboree (safari), Drakkar Noir 1000 Dunes Rally (4WD), Shell Festival Parade, Audi Driving Skills (driving challenge) and Federation Rally (4WD). For details, call EMSF (04 282 7111) or visit the website (emsfuae.org).

Clockwise from top left: Jet ski racing, having fun at a waterfall, scuba diving

Spectator Sports

Abu Dhabi has an exciting line-up of events for sport enthusiasts; from golf to motorsports, there should be plenty on offer to keep you entertained.

A wide range of sporting events are organised in Abu Dhabi and the emirate is backing an increasing number of international events. The UAE's sunny climate, its location within easy reach of Europe and Aisa, and its development of some excellent sporting facilities means the country is growing more attractive as a venue. Fans of live action can enjoy anything from motorsports at the Formula 1 Etihad Airways Abu Dhabi Grand Prix (p.59) to the Abu Dhabi Powerboat Championship (p.170) along the Corniche.

Camel Racing

Camel racing is a spectacular sport and it can be one of the most memorable highlights of any visit to the UAE. This traditional sport involves these ungainly animals being ridden around a track by robots, since the use of young child jockeys was banned. It has developed into a professional sport in the UAE with Dhs.25 million to be won as prize money each year. Races normally take place on weekend mornings during the winter months, with additional races on National Day and other public holidays.

Try to be at the racetracks early on a Friday morning to soak up the atmosphere. For a taste of this sport, head to the

Al Wathba Camel Race track, which is about 45 kilometres east of Abu Dhabi on the Al Ain road, or Al Maqam track near Al Ain. You will also have the opportunity to meet camel owners if you wish to know more about camel breeding and can bargain for some camel racing paraphernalia such as blankets, rugs and beads, or even buy a camel – they cost anything from Dhs.2,000 to Dhs.15,000. Entrance to the races is free of charge for spectators.

Golf

Abu Dhabi Golf Championship
Abu Dhabi Golf Club   www.abudhabigolfchampionship.com
With $2 million in prize money and some of the biggest names in golf, the annual Abu Dhabi Golf Championship is an important event in the emirate. Every January the European PGA Tour curtain-raiser is held at the Abu Dhabi Golf Club (02 558 8990, www.adgolfclub.com) which is renowned for its stunning course. Away from the action there is children's entertainment, competitions and food and beverage outlets, providing a fantastic family day out. Map 1 F4

Horse Racing

Abu Dhabi Equestrian Club   02 445 5500
Al Mushrif   www.adec-web.com
If you are looking for something different to do with your Sunday evening, the atmosphere of a race night is hard to beat. The season lasts from November to March and racing

takes place every Sunday night. The six races per meeting start every 30 minutes, from 18:00 (21:00 during Ramadan). Entry to the public area is free, as are the race cards. The Tri Cast Competition invites race goers to pick the first three finishers in each race. Entries must be submitted before the first race, and there are prizes for the winners. Children are allowed but must be supervised at all times. Refreshments are available and there are facilities for corporate hospitality. For further details, call 02 445 5500 or visit www.adec-web.com.
Map 1 C4

Motorsports

In 2009, Abu Dhabi hosted its first ever Formula 1 World Championship, held at the new Yas Island Marina Circuit in Abu Dhabi. The Formula 1 Etihad Airways Abu Dhabi Grand Prix was a high-profile three-day event which included concert performances from top acts including Beyoncé, Aerosmith and Kings of Leon. The Abu Dhabi Desert Challenge (www.uaedesertchallenge.com), which was previously known as the UAE Desert Challenge, is another popular event where motorbikes and 4WD's battle it out over the dunes.

Powerboat Racing

The Abu Dhabi Powerboat Championship is part of the 10 stage UIM F1 powerboat racing World Championship. The event in Abu Dhabi is a joint programme by Abu Dhabi and Sharjah featuring individual championship and team events. At this event, 20 to 24 boats representing 12 nations compete at high speed along the narrow, twisting course off the Corniche. The event is scheduled to take place in December. For more information go to www.f1h2o.com.

The Abu Dhabi International Marine Sports Club (02 681 5566) organises the annual President's Cup F2000 Powerboat Championship, the National Regatta, the National Jet-ski Championship, and the UAE Wooden Powerboat Championship, all of which are designed to encourage young Emiratis to remain close to their marine heritage. Each season also sees two open regattas for modern sailing boats (including catamarans, lasers and windsurfers), which are open to all ages and nationalities. ADIMSC also has a racing calendar, which runs from December to May; contact the race coordinator on adimsc@eim.ae for more information.

Tennis

Capitala World Tennis Championship

Abu Dhabi International Tennis
Complex, Zayed Sports City   www.capitalawtc.com

Abu Dhabi's first international tennis championship was held in January 2009. The event features family attractions as well as a series of tennis-based activities and tournaments during the run-up to the event, including the Community Cup. Top players, Roger Federer and Rafael Nadal played in the event which ran from the 31 December to 2 January 2010. The dates for the 2011 championship are yet to be announced.
Map 2 B2

Out Of Abu Dhabi

Although Abu Dhabi offers a plethora of ways to get active, head further afield and you'll find plenty more.

Dubai Desert Classic
04 380 2112

Emirates Golf Club   www.dubaidesertclassic.com

One of the highlights of the Dubai sporting calendar, this European PGA Tour competition is a popular event among both players and spectators at the end of January and start of February. Top golfers who have previously competed in the event include Tiger Woods and Ernie Elis.

Dubai Tennis Championships
04 282 4122

Dubai Tennis Stadium

www.barclaysdubaitennischampionships.com

The Dubai Tennis Championships takes place every February at the Aviation Club in Garhoud; it offers a great opportunity to catch some of the top players in the game at close quarters. The $1 million event is firmly established on the international tennis calendar, and features both men's and ladies' tournaments. Tickets for the later stages sell out in advance so keep an eye out for sale details – entrance to some of the earlier rounds can be bought on the day.

Dubai World Championship
04 365 8665

Jumeirah Golf Estates   www.dubaiworldchampionship.com

The Dubai World Championship is the grand finale of The Race to Dubai, the European Tour's season-long competition which features 50 tournaments in 27 destinations. This annual tournament runs for four days and is open to the leading 60 players in The Race to Dubai rankings after the 49th event, ensuring that the cream of the golf world qualify for the chance to compete for a prize fund of $7.5 million, with an additional $7.5 million bonus pool shared among the top 15 finishers.

Dubai World Cup
Meydan City

04 327 0000
www.dubaiworldcup.com

The buzzing atmosphere at the richest horse race in the world (last year's total prize money was more than $20 million), makes it one of the year's big social occasions. It has now moved from its previous location, Nad Al Sheba, to a new venue at Meydan City which opened in January 2010. You can see a slightly more raw form of horseracing at Jebel Ali racecourse (04 347 4914), near The Greens.

Emirates Airlines Dubai Rugby 7s
The Sevens, Al Ain Road

04 321 0008
www.dubairugby7s.com

One of the biggest fixtures in the UAE, the Dubai Rugby Sevens is a three-day event which plays host to the top 16 Sevens teams in the world. The first day of the event sees regional teams go head to head with the international teams joining the fray for the last two days. As well as the international matches, you can also watch social, youth and women's games at the event. Tickets for the Sevens regularly sell out weeks in advance so plan early. The event has moved to a larger facility called 'The Sevens' on Al Ain Road.

Spas

Arabian luxury extends to splendid spas that will transport you to paradise. If you want to feel like Cleopatra then you've come to the right place.

No luxury holiday is complete without a trip to the spa for a truly hedonistic head-to-toe pampering session. Whether you just fancy a facial or desire a day of indulgence you will find a wide variety of treatments on offer for the mind, body and face. From anti-ageing to body firming you will leave feeling like a new person. Unique to the region is the traditional Arabian treatment, the luxurious hammam experience, involving a full-body henna mask and some serious scrubbing – definitely not one for the inhibited!

Anantara Spa   02 690 7978
Emirates Palace   www.spa.anantara.com/abudhabi

The spa within Emirates Palace is just as elaborate and meticulously detailed as you would expect. The soft earth tones and gorgeous Arabesque decor will immediately relax any visitor and the treatment rooms are large and airy. Couple's treatments are available, including standard spa options as well as the signature hammam experience. Map 3 A2

Bodylines Health & Fitness Centre   02 697 9000
Various Locations   www.rotana.com

The menu here is limited to full body, hot stone or area specific massage, but the facility has a serene, spacious

Anantara Spa

layout. You can enjoy the steam room, sauna and Jacuzzi before your massage, which is a nice touch, and the therapist will offer a selection of fragrant oils for your treatment. Afterwards, relax on one of the day beds and prolong your feeling of Zen.

Bodylines is a Rotana brand: find branches at Beach Rotana (02 697 9000), Park Rotana (02 657 3333) and Yas Island Rotana (02 656 4000) and Al Ain Rotana (03 754 5111).

CHI, The Spa   02 509 8888
Shangri-La Qaryat Al Beri   www.shangri-la.com

The spa within the Shangri-La has quickly established itself as one of the most beautiful in the city. Covered in black marble, the treatment and relaxation rooms are quietly comfortable and relaxing. All the treatments you would expect from a high-end spa are available, and CHI prides itself on its half-day 'journeys' that include several treatments as well as lunch or dinner. Map 2 D2

Eden Spa & Health Club   02 644 6666
Le Meridien Abu Dhabi   www.starwoodhotels.com

The ultimate in stress relief and personal pampering, treatments include sessions in the aquamedic pool, various massages, aromatherapies, facials, mineral baths, seaweed wraps, and Turkish baths as well as its specialities of Lithos Therapy and Ayurveda. There is also a health club on-site, along with a tranquil beach and a variety of pools to relax in and around. Map 3 G3

Top: Bodylines Health & Fitness Centre; Bottom: Eden Spa & Health Club

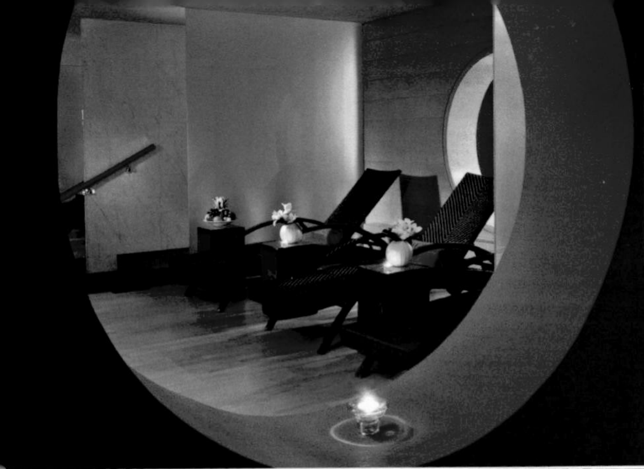

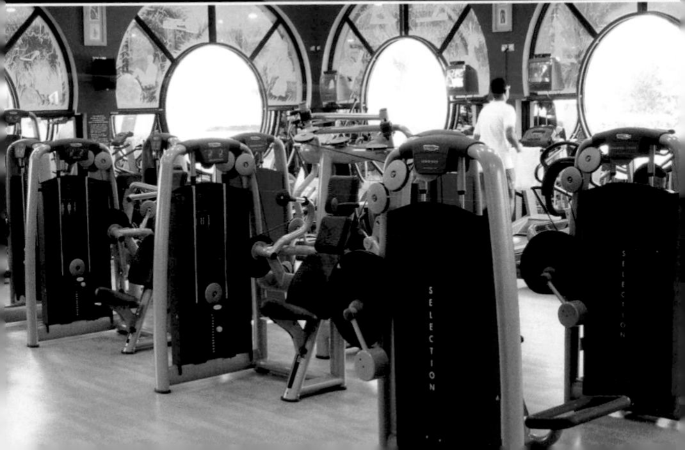
SELECTION
SELECTION

Hiltonia Health Club & Spa
Hilton Abu Dhabi

02 681 1900
www1.hilton.com

The Hiltonia Spa is a haven of tranquillity. Apart from the usual aromatherapy and reflexology treatments, it also offers Indian head massage and a range of hydro bath treatments. Alternatively, you can choose from a menu of special treatment packages, which combine body treatments, facials and nail care, and include the use of all spa facilities (sauna, eucalyptus steam room and Jacuzzi). **Map** 3 A2

Sisley Spa
Abu Dhabi Ladies Club

02 666 2228
www.adlc.ae

You don't have to be a member of the club to enjoy the finest treatments at this relaxing spa. It offers Balinese massage, acupressure and hot stone treatments, as well as an impressive range of facilities including a hydrobath, steam room and three treatment rooms. Check the website for monthly promotions. **Map** 3 D5

The SPA at Radisson Blu, Yas Island
Radisson Blu Hotel,
Abu Dhabi Yas Island

02 656 2000
www.radissonblu.com

Many of Abu Dhabi's spas reach exceptional levels, so factors like comfort and customer service take on extra importance. The SPA has them all down to an art. Arrive early and enjoy the Jacuzzi, steam room or sauna, then give your body over to the capable therapists. The aromatherapy massages and Anne Semonin facials are a cut above, but if you have time, try the luxurious signature Radisson Blu Formulation. **Map** 1 H3

Take time out at a luxurious spa

Zen Spa

02 697 9000

Beach Rotana Abu Dhabi

www.rotana.com

As spacious and comfortable a spa as you'll find anywhere, descending into ZEN is like disappearing down a rabbit hole of relaxation. If it can be scrubbed, wrapped, hydrated, treated or massaged, then it's on the menu, although the specific signature treatments, such as pregnancy, rejuvenation and immune boost massages are excellent value. Each room has character, and the tranquillity suites with private changing rooms, showers and colossal baths are luxury defined. **Map** 3 G4

Shopping

Capital Expenditure

From enormous malls selling modern marvels to traditional souks brimming with exotic treasures, Abu Dhabi's shopping scene is the epitome of variety.

The combination of Abu Dhabi's historical position on many ancient trade routes, and the mix of nationalities passing through the city today, make it a shopping destination of choice for bargain hunters, collectors, souvenir seekers and shopaholics alike. Not only will you find a huge selection of mainstream items, authentic antiques and some unusual discoveries, all at excellent prices, but with shops staying open late into the evenings you can really shop at leisure.

Carpets, gold, spices and wooden antiques are all hot items that find their way into many a homebound tourist's luggage. It's up to you whether you want to spend thousands on a genuine antique or finely woven silk carpet, or whether you want to use your pocket change to buy a few cheap souvenirs. Many stores can arrange to ship your purchases back to your home country.

The size and architecture of Abu Dhabi's malls can be a surprise to some visitors. These huge structures are spacious and fully air-conditioned, and packed with a range of international brands. Apart from everyday shops like supermarkets, clothing stores, card shops and electronics outlets, most malls also have several shops selling local souvenirs, carpets and perfume. Malls are much more than just places to shop equipped with a range of entertainment and leisure facilities; they are meeting points for families and friends – which make them perennially popular.

If you're after a more authentic Arabian shopping experience, head for the traditional markets, or souks (p.190). Apart from an eclectic range of goods for sale, the markets are great for photo opportunities and for the bustling atmosphere that you can see, hear and smell all at once. Items to look out for in the souks include spices, silks, perfumes, souvenirs and antiques. Often, shops specialising in certain products can be found side by side, so it's easy to compare prices. If you find a brand name item selling for an unbelievable price, it could well be a fake. Souks are usually open from 08:00 to 13:00 and 16:00 to 19:00, except Fridays when they only open in the afternoon.

Sizing

Figuring out your size is fairly straightforward. International sizes are often printed on garment labels or the store will usually have a conversion chart on display. Otherwise, a UK size is always two higher than a US size (so a UK 10 is a US 6). To convert European sizes into US sizes, subtract 32 (so a European 38 is actually a US 6). To convert European sizes into UK sizes, a 38 is roughly a 10. As for shoes, a woman's UK 6 is a European 39 or US 8.5 and a men's UK 10 is a European 44 or a US 10.5. If in doubt, ask for help.

Bargaining

Bargaining is still common practice in the souks and shopping areas of the UAE; you'll need to give it a go to get the best prices. Before you take the plunge, try to get an idea of prices from a few shops, as there can often be a significant difference. Once you've decided how much you are willing to spend, offer an initial bid that is roughly around half that price. Stay laidback and vaguely disinterested. When your initial offer is rejected (and it will be), keep going until you reach an agreement or until you have reached your limit. If the price isn't right, say so and walk out – the vendor will often follow and suggest a compromise price. The more you buy, the better the discount. When the price is agreed, it is considered bad form to back out of the sale.

While common in souks, bargaining isn't commonly accepted in malls and independent shops. However, use your discretion, as some shops such as jewellery stores, smaller electronics stores and eyewear optical centres do operate a set discount system and the price shown may be 'before discount'. Ask whether there is a discount on the marked price and you may end up with a bargain.

Shipping

Fortunately, many courier and shipping companies have spotted the opportunity to service those who have forgotten about airport baggage restrictions and offer good deals on shipping your booty back home. You have the option of sending goods by airmail, courier or sea; for smaller items, or for those that have to be delivered quickly, air freight is better and the items can be tracked. Aramex (www.aramex.com), DHL (www.dhl.co.ae), Federal Express (www.fedex.com), TNT (www.tnt.com) and UPS (www.ups.com) are all present in Abu Dhabi.

Clockwise from top: Arabian lanterns, pottery, colourful painted tiles

Where To Go For...

Art

While there's nowhere like the Tate Gallery or the Louvre in Abu Dhabi (well, not yet anyway), there are a few art galleries that have interesting exhibitions of art and traditional Arabic artefacts. The Folklore Gallery (02 666 0361) is a great place for browsing, with displays of local pottery and art, and for having framing done; there's a wide range of frames and the craftsmanship is high. Hemisphere Design Studio & Gallery (02 676 8614, www.hemisphere.ae) is an independent gallery that holds exhibitions showcasing the work of local artists, and it also runs courses. If you're up for a bit of a drive, it is worth visiting the Sharjah Art Museum (06 568 8222, www.sharjahmuseums.ae).

Carpets

Abu Dhabi boasts a huge range of carpets, which are available in various colours, designs, materials and prices. Traditionally, carpets come from Iran, Pakistan, Turkey, China and Central Asia. While salesmen are generally helpful and honest, it helps if you know a little bit about carpets before you agree on a price. As a rough guide, the higher the number of knots per square inch, the higher the price and the better the quality. Handmade carpets also fetch a higher price.

Most vendors will happily unroll carpet after carpet, discussing its history and merits at length. Don't feel obliged to purchase just because he has broken a sweat, but if you do want to buy, stick to your budget and bargain as hard as you can.

Gold

The UAE is justifiably known as one of the best places in the world to buy gold, and the capital leads the way. Gold in Abu Dhabi is sold according to the fixed daily international gold rate, which is not up for negotiation. However, when buying a piece of jewellery a charge is added for craftsmanship and this is where your bargaining power increases. A popular souvenir is to have your name in Arabic made into a gold pendant; most jewellery shops offer this service in white or yellow gold.

There are jewellery shops in most malls, but if you want the best range and more room to bargain, head to either Hamdan Street near the Liwa Centre, or to the Madinat Zayed Shopping Centre & Gold Centre (p.202).

Souvenirs

You may find items for sale, such as ivory, which are subject to international trade and import bans or contravene the CITES convention. Don't risk taking them with you. If you wish to buy souvenirs that promote and preserve local handicrafts, and don't break the law, see the companies listed at Made in the UAE (www.madeintheuae.com). Colourful pashminas are widely available and they are great as lightweight shawls (for when the weather is warm but the air conditioning is cold). While genuine pashminas are made from the wool of the pashmina goat (found only in Kashmir, India), most pashminas today are made of a cotton or silk mix, and the ratio dictates the price. Souvenir shops usually have several shelves stacked high with a kaleidoscope of colours. Compare prices in a few shops to get a feel for quality and range, and have a go at bargaining before you agree on a price.

Shisha pipes are widely available in souvenir shops and hypermarkets, and the tobacco comes in a variety of flavours. Wooden trinket boxes, photo frames and carvings are popular and can be found in souvenir shops. They are often decorated with brass or polished camel bone. The Hamdan Centre (p.199) has an excellent range of shoes and handbags at bargain prices, should you fancy a spree.

Tailoring

There are so many tailors in Abu Dhabi and most operate from small shops tucked away down side streets. It is well worth buying a few metres of fabric and getting something made up to your measurements – tailors can copy a pattern, a garment, or even a photograph. Standards of workmanship vary, so ask around to get recommendations of good tailors.

Most tailors have a stack of fashion catalogues that you can look through to get some ideas, and once you've chosen something they will be able to tell you how much fabric you need to buy. They will probably provide the little extras like zips, buttons and cotton.

Confirm the price before the tailor starts working on the item. In most cases you'll find that the cost of having something made is very reasonable, although it obviously depends on the intricacy of the workmanship required. When the garment is finished, you will be able to try it on and have minor adjustments made if necessary.

Shopping for luxurious items

Souks & Markets

These traditional markets have evolved from dusty hubs of trade into bustling tourist attractions packed with a fascinating collection of items.

Souk is the Arabic word for a market or a place where any kind of goods are bought or exchanged. Historically, dhows from the Far East, China, Ceylon and India would offload their cargo, and the goods would be haggled over in the souks adjacent to the docks. Souks were the social and commercial centre of life here, providing a place to meet friends and socialise outside the family.

Over the years the items on sale have diversified dramatically from spices, silks and perfumes, to include electronic goods and the latest kitsch consumer trends.

Keep The Khanjar

If you buy a khanjar (traditional dagger), it will need to be packed in your luggage to go in the hold – even if it's been framed – and you may still need to declare it. If you try to carry it in your hand luggage it will be confiscated.

Traditionally, the souks developed organically and were a maze of shady alleyways, with small shops opening on to the paths. Nowadays most of these have been redesigned and replaced by large, air-conditioned developments. Although Abu Dhabi's souks aren't as fascinating as others in the Arab world, such as Fes in Morocco or Mutrah in Oman, they are worth a visit for their bustling atmosphere, eclectic variety of goods, and the traditional way of doing business. Some of the souks have porters who will follow you around and carry your goods for a few dirhams (agree on a price though, before they start).

The Central Market (p.191) in Abu Dhabi is currently undergoing redevelopment. It will transform the area from the eclectic mix of small traders that it was, into a modern centrepiece for the city, with hotels, apartments and an Arabian souk area – probably not the same sort of shops as were there originally though. Many of the traders have moved into the nearby Fish Souk or to the Madinat Zayed Shopping Centre.

Al Ain Central Market
East of Jebel Hafeet
One of the only camel markets left in the UAE, this is a great way to experience a bit of local trading, while camel blankets make great souvenirs. The market now also contains the livestock market. **Map** 4 H9

Al Ain Souk
Zayed Bin Sultan St, Al Ain
Also known as the Central or Old Souk, the Al Ain Souk is a great place to explore, savour the local atmosphere, and practise your bargaining skills. The souk itself is a rather ramshackle affair but makes a refreshing change from many of the modern, rather sterile, air-conditioned markets that are appearing elsewhere across the Emirates. **Map** 4 G8

Carpet Souk

Al Meena Street, Al Meena

Yemeni mattresses and machine-made carpets dominate, but bargains can be found if you know what you're looking for so don't forget to haggle. Some of the vendors will make Arabic 'majlis' cushions to order for a very reasonable price. This is also known as the Afghan Souk and is located on Al Meena Street near the main port area. **Map** 3 H2

Fish, Fruit & Vegetable Souk

Nr Iranian Souk, Al Meena

Fish doesn't get much fresher than this. The day's catch is loaded onto the quayside and sold wholesale for the first two hours of trading (04:30 to 06:30), with smaller quantities sold after that. The atmosphere is electric and trading is conducted the same way it has been for many years. The Fruit & Vegetable Souk across the road is a more relaxed place where an amazing range of produce can be bought by the box or the kilo. Go early for the freshest produce. **Map** 3 H1

Iranian Souk

Nr Fish, Fruit & Vegetable Souk, Al Meena

It may not be air-conditioned, but this souk is worth a visit for the fresh batches of Iranian goods which arrive regularly by dhow or barge. Everything is on sale, from household goods and terracotta urns, to decorative metal, cane and glass items. It's also a great place for plants – both indoor and outdoor. Also known as Al Meena Souk. **Map** 3 H1

Top: handicrafts and furniture on sale at the Iranian Souk; Bottom: a shop in the Carpet Souk

Mwaifa Souk
Sheikh Khalifa Bin Zayed St, Al Ain

This modern market consists of a long strip of handy shops, with an intriguing mix of chain stores and independents. including a bakery, a baby shop and a toy shop. **Map** 4 E8

Souk Al Zaafarana
03 762 1868

Al Khubaisi, Al Ain

Al Zaafaranah Souk is one of the largest and most popular in Al Ain. With more than 150 shops – the fruit and vegetable market alone has more than 90 shops – it offers a beguiling range of textiles, hand-crafted goods and perfumes. There is also a seafood restaurant and kids' play area. **Map** 4 F7

Souk Qaryat Al Beri > *p.195*
02 558 1670

Btn Maqtaa & Musaffah Bridges, Bain Al Jessrain

This modern-day souk is a magnificent example of Arabian architecture and a first of its kind in the capital. The area holds a mix of local and international retail brands, coffee shops and a diverse range of restaurants. Abras wind through the canals providing transportation around the souk and the stunning complex offers stunning alfresco dining options. **Map** 2 D1

Souk Al Bawadi & Al Qaws
Zayed Bin Sultan St, Al Ain

Connected to Bawadi Mall, these two markets offer a good selection. Souk Al Bawadi has a heritage feel with stores selling traditional items and souvenirs. Souk Al Qaws has practical shops including banks and money exchanges. **Map** 4 G8

سوق قرية البري

THE SOUK AT QARYAT AL BERI

Shopping Malls

The most popular malls are more than just places to shop; in the evenings, and especially at the weekends, they are places to meet, eat and parade.

Abu Dhabi Co-operative Society
02 678 1999

Sheikh Zayed 1st St · www.adcoops.com

This shopping centre has been around for some time; its main draws are Splash (trendy, inexpensive fashions), Shoe Mart (huge range of shoes), Lifestyle (funky gifts and much more) and The Baby Shop. Other smaller shops include computer suppliers and ladies' fashion outlets. **Map** 3 C5

Abu Dhabi Mall
02 645 4858

Tourist Club Street · www.abudhabi-mall.com

This is one of the main attractions of the Abu Dhabi shopping scene. With over 200 retail outlets spread over four floors, it attracts over 25,000 visitors each day. It's range of international highstreet stores and local brands should keep most shopaholics happy. Abu Dhabi Mall is not just a shopping destination – with restaurants on every floor, a nine-screen cineplex, a huge food court and even a children's play area, there is something to keep the whole family happy. It also hosts exciting promotional exhibitions throughout the year, including a popular Christmas Market. The mall has a sizeable carpark and a large branch of Abu Dhabi Co-op can be found on the ground floor. **Map** 3 G3

Abu Dhabi Mall

Al Ain Mall

03 766 0333

Al Qwaitat St, Al Ain   www.alainmall.net

Al Ain Mall has changed the face of shopping in the 'garden city'. With over 100,000 square metres of retail and entertainment space spread over three floors, this bright, modern mall has stores selling a wide range of souvenirs, jewellery and every-day items. The family entertainment area has a 12 lane bowling alley as well as a multi-screen cinema and there is an ice-skating rink on the ground floor. **Map** 4 H8

Al Jimi Mall

03 763 8883

Government Road, Al Ain   www.aljimimall.com

This bright and airy single storey mall is not huge, but attracts plenty of custom. It is anchored by Carrefour (the French hypermarket chain) and, with over 70 stores to choose from, there's plenty of shopping to be had. The mall's range of retail outlets includes Splash, Shoe Mart, Home Centre and The Baby Shop. There's a good selection of food outlets and a large entertainment area to keep the kids busy. **Map** 4 F7

Al Wahda Mall

02 443 7000

Shk Hazza Bin Zayed Street   www.alwahda-mall.com

With more than 150 shops, a hypermarket and foodcourt, Al Wahda is an impressive addition to Abu Dhabi's retail landscape. The mall covers more than 1.5 million square feet and features fashion, electronics, jewellery and health and beauty stores across two floors. There is parking for more than 1,500 cars. **Map** 3 E5

Bawadi Mall

03 784 0000

Zayed Bin Sultan Road, Al Ain · www.bawadimall.com

The Bawadi Mall has set high standards for the city's shopping scene. Browse through 400 shops, representing both international and regional brands and a range of high street and designer names. For refreshment, head to the food court or one of the many casual dining outlets throughout the mall. There is also entertainment for the family including a ski village, rollercoaster, an eight-screen cinema and a bowling alley. The Heritage Village features beautiful Islamic architecture and a range of shops selling souvenirs in a traditional market. The mall also has two outdoor markets, Souk Al Bawadi and Al Qaws. **Map** F G8

Fotouh Al Khair Centre

02 681 1130

Rashid Bin Saeed Al Maktoum St

This is home to some of the world's favourite brands including Marks & Spencer and Monsoon. With a host of other outlets selling everything from watches to lingerie and children's fashions, this mall buzzes in the evenings and at the weekends. **Map** 3 E3

Hamdan Centre

02 632 8555

Shk Hamdan Bin Mohd St

Something of an institution on Abu Dhabi's shopping scene and located in the heart of the city, this vibrant centre is a good place to buy clothing, leather, shoes, sports equipment and touristy knick-knacks, all at reasonable prices. Practise your bargaining skills here to get a good discount. **Map** 3 E2

Khalidiyah Mall

02 635 4000
26th Street
www.khalidiyahmall.com

The mall should not to be confused with the older, smaller Khalidiyah Centre just up the road. It is designed in a distinctive Islamic architectural style and is spread out over three floors. Home to over 160 stores, a large branch of Lulu Hypermarket (p.202) can be found on the first and second floors. Other highlights include UK department stores, Debenhams and BHS, plentiful cafes and restaurants and a large foodcourt. The third floor offers a few entertainment options: Sparky's Family Fun Centre (02 635 4317) is an amusement centre which includes rides and a bowling alley, and the nine-screen CineRoyal cinema. **Map** 3 C3

Khalifa Centre

Nr Abu Dhabi Co-operative Society, Tourist Club Area

This mall is teeming with regional craft and souvenir shops, as well as outlets selling Persian and Baluchi carpets. It's an essential stop if you're looking for souvenirs but would rather not visit the souks. **Map** 3 C5

Liwa Centre

Shk Hamdan Bin Mohd St

This is where to head on Hamdan Street for jewellery, clothes, makeup, perfume and more. It's a spot where men and women can get glammed up on the cheap. Book lovers should head for House of Prose, an excellent second-hand bookshop. Be sure to visit the vibrant foodcourt on the second level. **Map** 3 E2

Clockwise from top left: Al Ain Mall, Madinat Zayed Shopping Centre & Gold Centre, Marina Mall

Lulu Center
Salam Street

02 678 0707
www.luluhypermarket.com

This is an Aladdin's cave selling everything under the sun –
from electronics, sportswear and toys, to stationery, clothing,
cosmetics and travel accessories. Some items are real
bargains, some are pretty tatty, but prices are reasonable.
Map 1 C3

Madinat Zayed Shopping Centre & Gold Centre
Corniche Road East

02 631 8555

Shopaholics will love this mall – it has over 400 outlets selling
just about everything; some of the traders from the Central
Souk have relocated here. Next to the main mall, Homes r Us
is popular for furniture and home accessories. Japanese store
Daiso has an eclectic range of stock and most items are Dhs.6.
The Madinat Zayed Gold Centre, adjacent to the main mall,
glitters with the finest gold, diamond and pearl jewellery. The
supervised toddlers' area and the games arcade will keep the
kids entertained while you shop. **Map** 3 E3

Marina Mall
Breakwater

02 681 8300
www.marinamall.ae

Situated on the Breakwater, Marina Mall is one of Abu
Dhabi's biggest shopping centres and offers plenty of
entertainment options. It houses a tower with a viewing
platform and restaurant, a nine-screen Cinestar complex, Fun
City amusement centre for the kids and an icerink. There are
a host of stores including luxury brands such as Louis Vuitton

Souvenirs with regional flavour

and Fendi, plus several restaurants, fastfood outlets and coffee shops. **Map** 3 B1

MultiBrand
02 621 9700

Jct Hamdan & Najda St

This large, open-plan location is home to well-known international shops. Its store list sounds like it has come straight from a British high street, with shops such as Mothercare, Claire's, Next and Oasis. For footwear there's the stylish Milano. **Map** 3 F3

Rotana Mall
02 681 4433

Al Khaleej Al Arabi Street

Near the Corniche, this dinky mall is best known for a few shops selling antiques, carpets, handicrafts, Arabic pottery and wall hangings. There are some nice pieces here. **Map** 3 C3

Department Stores

Marks & Spencer
Fotouh Al Khair Centre

02 621 3646
www.marksandspencerme.com

One of the best known brands from the UK, M&S, as it is known, sells men's, women's and children's clothes and shoes, along with a small, but ever popular, selection of food. The store is famous for its selection of underwear and has a reputation for quality. It's also a great place to stock up on basics. Branches in the UAE carry selected ranges which include the Per Una range – high street chic – as well as more classic lines. **Map** 3 E3

Next
Various Locations

02 645 4832
www.next.co.uk

Next is a popular British chain that now has a number of stores in the UAE. Each branch stocks a range of quality high-street fashion for men, women and children, as well as shoes, underwear and accessories. It's a great place to go clothes shopping for all occasions, whether you need casual daywear, office attire, party outfits or even semi-formal evening wear. The kids' clothing section is excellent catering for newborns to teenagers and has a good range of children's shoes.

Studio R
Marina Mall

02 681 7676
www.rshlimited.com

Studio R sells a selection of brands catering to those with an active lifestyle. With a range of well-known clothing labels (Mango, Bebe, Massimo Dutti, Tag Heuer, Lacoste and Rockport), and sports brands (Adidas, New Balance and

Reebok), Studio R has created its own niche. Look out for sales throughout the year, when prices are heavily discounted.
Map 3 B1

Woolworths
02 681 0881
Marina Mall
www.woolworths.co.za

This is a home away from home for South Africans – Woolworths in South Africa is similar to Marks & Spencer in the UK. It is renowned as the place to go for high-quality clothes, shoes and home textiles (towels and bedding). They also do a great range of accessories and underwear. In the UAE, Woolworths may be slightly less impressive than the original stores, but the items are still high quality and the range offers something a little different to standard (UK) goods. **Map** 3 B1

Supermarkets & Hypermarkets

Abu Dhabi has a good range of stores and supermarkets stocking a wide selection of international and local produce. Prices vary dramatically; produce is imported from all over the world and some items cost twice as much as they would in their country of origin. There are plenty of 'corner shops' in residential areas, good for last-minute essentials. Popular food shops include the Abu Dhabi Co-operative Society (www.adcoops.com), which has branches all over the city, and Al Ahlia Prisunic – often simply known as Prisunic (www.alahliagroup.com). Abela is a superstore with a range of shops inside offering stationery, video rental, books and magazines, dry-cleaning services and jewellery (and much more). In terms of food, Abela is a western-style supermarket with a pork section and a good fresh fish counter. Spinneys (www.spinneys.co.ae) keeps the Brits happy with its Waitrose range as well as other British products, but the store also stocks a great range of South African, Australian and American products. Carrefour (www.carrefouruae.com) is a huge hypermarket and part of a large French chain. It sells everything from cheap shoes to toothpaste, as well as a good selection of fruit, vegetables, fish and seafood.

Independent & Noteworthy Shops

Abu Dhabi's independent scene isn't as varied as some cities, but there are a few stores dotted around that generate interest. Souk Qaryat Al Beri (p.194) has a few independent outlets that are worth exploring. La Casa Del Habano (02 644 1505) in Abu Dhabi Mall is worth a visit if you are after a hit of tobacco – you'll can also find shisha paraphernalia here.

Unapologetically girlie, S*uce (02 681 8650, www.shopatsauce.com) is a haven for those who like things chic with a feminine touch. Funky accessories, quirky fashion and individual pieces are the hallmark of this boutique in the Marina Mall.

Ounass (which means 'people' in Arabic) is another store that appeals to the sophisticated party people of the UAE. It stocks lines from high-end designers such as Marchesa and Alberta Ferretti. The store has a branch in Marina Mall (02 681 8300).

Big Spenders

With the varied choice of local treasures and shopping pleasures you may find your purchases exceed your luggage allowance. Fortunately, many courier and shipping companies offer visitors good deals on shipping your booty back home. You can send goods by airmail, courier or sea; options include: Aramex (02 555 1911, www.aramex.com), DHL (800 4004, www.dhl.co.ae) and Federal Express (800 33339, www.fedex.com/ae).

Shopping for jewels

Going Out

After Hours

Visitors should be pleasantly surprised with the night life in the emirate, whether you want to soak up the atmosphere or enjoy the party.

Cosmopolitan and bustling, Abu Dhabi has an excellent and ever-increasing variety of restaurants. From Moroccan to Mexican, Indian to Italian and everything in between, there really is something to suit every palate and budget.

Many of Abu Dhabi's best and most popular restaurants are located in hotels. These are pretty much the only outlets that can serve alcohol with your meal, although some clubs and associations are also permitted to do so. The taxes levied on alcohol translate into fairly high prices for drinks at a restaurant. You will rarely find a bottle of house wine for less than around Dhs.90, and a beer will probably cost you at least Dhs.20 but often

The Yellow Star
The little yellow star highlights venues that merit extra praise. It could be the atmosphere, the food, the cocktails, the music or the crowd, but whatever the reason, any review that you see with the star attached is somewhere considered a bit special.

more. However, there are quite a number of unlicensed independent restaurants throughout town that are excellent and shouldn't be ignored. 'Tourist' restaurants, mainly those located in hotels, are permitted to charge service fees. Tax and service charges can add an extra 16% to the bill so, to avoid a nasty surprise, check the small print on the menu to see whether these charges are included in the prices. If you want to reward the waiting staff directly then the standard rule of a 10% tip will be appreciated.

The capital may not have the quantity of outlets of a big city like New York, but there's plenty of variety to keep even the most ardent socialite happy.

People tend to go out late in Abu Dhabi and usually not before 21:00. Even on weeknights, kick off is surprisingly late. If you're venturing out to Arabic nightclubs or restaurants before 23:00, you're likely to find them almost deserted, but new bars like Pearls & Caviar (p.259) are boosting business.

Generally, cafes and restaurants close between 23:00 and 01:00, and most bars and nightclubs split between those who close 'early' at 01:00 and those who stay open 'late' until 02:00 or 03:00. Few are open all night.

Brunch & Other Deals

An integral part of life in the capital, the famous Friday brunch is a perfect event for a lazy start to the weekend, especially once the hot weather arrives. Popular with all sections of the community, it provides Thursday night's revellers with a gentle awakening and some much needed nourishment. For families, brunch is a pleasant way to spend the earlier part of the day, especially since many venues organise a variety of fun activities for kids, allowing parents to fill themselves with fine food and drink, and to simply relax with friends.

Thursday and Friday nights are obviously busy, but you will also find that during the week many bars and restaurants offer promotions and special nights to attract customers, thus creating a lively atmosphere. Particularly popular is ladies' night, which is the busiest night of the week for some places (usually Tuesday night, but it varies from place to place). Women are given drink tokens at the door and the number varies from one to an endless supply, though it may be limited to certain types of drinks. This ploy certainly seems to attract male customers too.

Vegetarian

Vegetarians should be pleasantly surprised by the range and variety of veggie food that can be found in restaurants in Abu Dhabi. Although the main course of Arabic cuisine is dominated by meat, the staggering range of mezze (which are often vegetarian) and the general affection for fresh vegetables should offer enough variety to satisfy even the most ravenous herbivore.

Most outlets offer at least one or two veggie dishes. However, if you want a little more variety, choices include the numerous Indian vegetarian restaurants catering to the large number of Indians who are vegetarian by religion (see Indian on p.221). These offer diverse styles of cooking and a range of tasty dishes – for vegetarians, this option is hard to beat. Other highlights include loads of excellent Italian (p.222),

Mexican (p.222) and international restaurants (p.221) all over the city. Some of Abu Dhabi's cafes serve good vegetarian food, especially THE One (p.271).

A word of warning: if you are a strict veggie, confirm that your meal is completely meat free. Some restaurants cook their vegetarian selection with animal fat or on the same grill as the meat dishes.

Nightclubs

Abu Dhabi's nightclubs are busy from about 23:00 till the wee hours. The city has a reasonable number of dedicated nightclubs as well as numerous other venues that have schizophrenic personalities (bars or restaurants earlier in the

evening, and later turning into a packed joint where you can cut loose on the dancefloor). If you want to indulge in some authentic clubbing, head to the neighbouring emirate of Dubai, which is frequently visited by international DJs.

Additionally, since you're in the Middle East, do not overlook the option of Arabic nightclubs. This is your chance to sample Arabic cuisine and enjoy a night of traditional entertainment, usually with a belly dancer, a live band and a singer. These venues start buzzing very late in the evening – a classic reflection of the Arabic way of starting late and finishing, well… later.

Street Food

Throughout the city, you will find roadside stands selling 'shawarma' (made from rolled pita bread filled with lamb or chicken that is carved from a rotating spit) and salad. Costing about Dhs.3 each, this is not only an inexpensive option but also well worth trying as an

Door Policy

There are few considerations to heed when going out in Abu Dhabi: anyone who is rowdy may find their entry is refused (and drunken behaviour in public places can land you behind bars); large groups, single men and certain nationalities may have difficulty gaining admission, but breaking the group up or by going in a mixed gender group can help. The minimum drinking age is 21.

excellent alternative to the usual hamburger. Shawarma stands usually sell other dishes too, such as 'foul' (a paste made from fava beans) and 'falafel' (or ta'amiya), small savoury balls of deep fried chickpeas. And if it's value for money you're after, for just Dhs.11, you can buy a whole grilled chicken, salad and hummus.

While most shawarma stands offer virtually the same thing, slight differences make some stand out from the rest. People are often adamant that their particular favourite serves, for example, the best falafel in town. These stands are often the first place where you eat when you come to the UAE. Every restaurant has its own way of doing things and you might find that the best place is, surprisingly, the smallest, most low key restaurant you happened upon by chance.

Arabian Experience

There are ample opportunities to enjoy traditional Arabic cuisine. Most of Abu Dhabi's cuisine hails from Lebanon and Syria. Tabouleh (chopped parsley with bulgar, tomato and herbs), fattoush (tangy salad seasoned with sumac and topped with toasted pita), aryaas (grilled flat bread with spiced meat in the middle) and many kinds of grilled, skewered meat can be found in any Arabic restaurant and are great introductions to local cuisine (p.220).

The full Arabian experience can be enjoyed in the desert, on a safari, where you will be entertained by a belly dancer, smoke shisha and dine on a full array of Arabic delights under the stars. Most tour operators (p.152) offer a desert dinner experience.

Entertainment

The variety of entertainment in Abu Dhabi is growing with an annual film festival and international music acts now major parts of the events calendar.

Cinema

A trip to the cinema is one of the most popular forms of entertainment in the Emirates and movie buffs are relatively well catered for, although showings are generally limited to the latest Arabic, Asian or Hollywood films.

Most of the bigger cinemas, CineStar (www.cinestarcinemas.com) and Grand Cinemas (www.grandcinemas.com), are multi-screen mega sites, while the older cinemas tend to have fewer screens. Both companies have several branches in Al Ain and Abu Dhabi. For movie times, check the daily newspapers as well as *Entertainment Plus*, the weekly magazine that is published with *Gulf News* every Wednesday. A handy website for checking movies and show times is http://movies.theemiratesnetwork.com.

Movie release dates vary considerably with new Hollywood films reaching the UAE from anywhere between four weeks to a year after release in the United States.

Inside, the air conditioners are usually on high and it can become very cold, so make sure you take something warm to wear. At weekends, there are extra shows at midnight or 01:00 – check the press for details. Tickets can be reserved, but usually have to be collected an hour before the show and sales are cash only. However, with so many screens around now, you will often find cinemas half empty, except for the first couple of days after the release of an eagerly awaited blockbuster.

Abu Dhabi Film Festival (p.58) is a big highlight on the cultural calendar and cinema screenings and events include a great selection of international films. In 2010, the film festival is planned for 14 to 23 October.

Comedy

The regular comedy scene in Abu Dhabi is, unfortunately, quite limited. However, there are regular visits from Dubai-based company, The Laughter Factory (04 355 1862, www. thelaughterfactory.com), as well as the occasional comical theatre production or one-off event. Comedy shows tend to be aimed at the British population, so other nationalities may not always get the joke. Events are often promoted only a short time before they actually take place, so keep your ears to the ground for what's coming up.

Live Music

There is no regular calendar of events for music lovers in Abu Dhabi, although recent years have seen a slight upturn in the music scene. At different times of the year (mainly in winter), major sporting events, concerts and festivals feature international artists, bands and classical musicians.

The opening of the Emirates Palace (p.68) has brought a new concert venue to Abu Dhabi's music scene and a number of international artists have played there including Shakira,

George Michael, Alicia Keyes, Bon Jovi, Justin Timberlake, Christina Aguillera and Coldplay. Club events, such as Ministry of Sound nights, have also taken place in Abu Dhabi, and the Abu Dhabi Music & Arts Foundation (www.admaf.org) has hosted several cultural events. The Abu Dhabi Classics programme which runs throughout the winter months is well attended (www.abudhabi-classics.ae). Moreover, the ever popular Jazz Festival in November and Latino Festival in March (organised by Chillout Productions, 04 391 1196) are annual events that are not to be missed. Also worth noting is WOMAD, Peter Gabriel's 'World of Music and Dance' festival, which has become an annual fixture, since 2009, held in April on Abu Dhabi Corniche and at Al Jahili Fort in Al Ain. Public admission is free to much of the festival (www.womadabudhabi.ae).

Promoters rarely have long term programmes and details are only available about a month in advance, so for details of events, check the daily press or monthly magazines, including Explorer's *Live Work Explore*.

Theatre

The theatre scene in Abu Dhabi is rather quiet, with fans relying chiefly on touring companies and the occasional amateur dramatics performance. The amateur theatre, namely the Abu Dhabi Drama Society (www.the-club.com/drama), always welcomes new members either on stage or behind the scenes. There is also the occasional murder mystery dinner where you are encouraged to display your thespian skills by being part of the performance.

WOMAD Abu Dhabi

Venue Directory

Cafes & Restaurants

Bars, Pubs & Clubs

Al Ain
Restaurant

Bars

Al Meena & Tourist Club Area
Restaurant

Le Bistrot	Le Meridien Abu Dhabi	p.252
Pappagallo	Le Meridien Abu Dhabi	p.259
Prego's	Beach Rotana Abu Dhabi	p.259
Riviera	Tourist Club Area	p.260
Rock Bottom Café	Al Diar Capital Hotel	p.262
Rodeo Grill	Beach Rotana Abu Dhabi	p.262
The Alamo	Abu Dhabi Marina & Yacht Club	p.267
The Restaurant	The Club	p.268
The Village Club	One To One Hotel – The Village	p.271
Trader Vic's	Beach Rotana Abu Dhabi	p.272
Zest	The Club	p.274

Bars

Captain's Arms	Le Meridien Abu Dhabi	p.276
Colosseum	Abu Dhabi Marina & Yacht Club	p.276
LAB – Lounge At The Beach	Beach Rotana Abu Dhabi	p.278

Bain Al Jessrain & Al Raha Beach

Restaurant

Asian Bistro & Sushi Bar	Abu Dhabi Golf Club	p.236
Bord Eau	Shangri-La Hotel Qaryat Al Beri	p.238
Elements	Fairmont Bab Al Bahr	p.244
Hoi An	Shangri-La Hotel Qaryat Al Beri	p.247
Pearls & Caviar	Shangri-La Hotel Qaryat Al Beri	p.259
Sevilla	Al Raha Beach Hotel	p.264
Shang Palace	Shangri-La Hotel Qaryat Al Beri	p.264

Corniche East & Central Abu Dhabi

Restaurant

Corniche West

Restaurant

Bars

Ras Al Akhdar & Breakwater

Restaurant

Restaurants & Cafes

From top-notch fine dining and swanky bars to independent eateries and fast food joints, there is a vast selection of eating options on offer in the emirate.

18Oz
One To One Hotel – The Village

Steakhouse
02 495 2000

18Oz specialises in mouth-watering steaks and chops, serving choice cuts of Angus beef drenched in a selection of eight sauces. Seafood appetisers and lamb, chicken and vegetarian main dishes can also be found on the menu. The modern decor and attentive service feels just right, and even the deserts are delicious. **Map** 3 F6

49er's The Gold Rush
Al Diar Dana Hotel

American
02 645 6000

Centrally situated, this popular venue is often packed so get there early to enjoy an entire evening of entertainment. The rich timber finishes reflect a traditional ranch-style atmosphere and the food is delicious, with steaks that melt in the mouth. The service cannot be faulted and, with live music and reasonable prices, you can't go too wrong. **Map** 3 G3

Al Arish
Nr Mina Fish Market, Al Meena

Emirati
02 673 2266

For an authentic Arabian experience, look no further. At Al Arish, guests are instantly welcomed and assisted in choosing

Business on the beach.
Discover the Fairmont experience.

Set at the gateway to Abu Dhabi on the creek side beach-front,
Fairmont Bab Al Bahr offers the highest level of elegance and comfort
throughout its 369 luxuriously appointed guest rooms and suites and a
variety of captivating dining venues.

Introduce yourself to a century of service excellence as you check into
the new Fairmont Bab Al Bahr.

For reservations or more information, please call **+971 2 654 3000**
or toll free (UAE) **800 848 000**, email **babalbahr.reservations@fairmont.com**
or visit **www.fairmont.com/babalbahr**

from the attractive buffet selection of seafood, chicken and meat. Food at this restaurant is extremely fresh and plentiful. A healthy choice of 'local' and traditional starters, mains and desserts can be washed down with freshly made fruit cocktails that are highly recommended. This is definitely a hidden gem. **Map** 3 H1

Al Birkeh
Arabic
Le Meridien Abu Dhabi   02 644 6666
Widely touted as one of the best Arabic restaurants in town, this established venue serves traditional Middle Eastern fare in a festive setting, complete with live music and a belly dancer. Start your culinary journey with a selection of hot and cold mezze before moving on to your main course of grilled meat or fish (and lots of it!). For the gastronomically brave only, the menu includes some exotic dishes such as raw liver, washed down with the strong aniseed drink 'arak'. **Map** 3 G3

Al Datrah Restaurant
Emirati
Heritage Village   02 681 4455
This traditional cafe is a must. Where else can you stand under a windtower to test the earliest form of air conditioning while you sip on fresh fruit cocktails? You can also marvel at the contrast between the authentic artefacts of a bygone age and the glistening, ultra-modern cityscape across the turquoise waters on the Corniche. The menu features typical Arabic fare, with a buffet in the evenings. **Map** 3 C1

18Oz

Al Dhafra

Dinner Cruise
02 673 2266

Nr Mina Fish Market, Al Meena

This traditional dhow offers daily dinner cruises along the picturesque corniche. The upper deck boasts a majlis and the lower air-conditioned deck can seat approximately 50 people. A sumptuous menu includes lavish Arabic fare, and as you dine, the ethnic charm of the dhow and the serenity of the placid Arabian waters will ensure an unforgettable evening. **Map** 3 H1

Al Fanar

International
02 674 2020

Le Royal Meridien Abu Dhabi

Professional, polite waiters who cater to your every whim, enhance the feeling of other-worldliness at this revolving rooftop restaurant. The magnificent panoramic views

are almost eclipsed by the extravagantly elaborate feast that is set before you. The hushed atmosphere and plush furnishings provide the perfect opportunity for gazing at stars or into a loved one's eyes. Al Fanar offers a truly impressive feast and a chance to see the city lights and Corniche from a unique angle. **Map** 2 F2

Amalfi
Le Royal Meridien Abu Dhabi

Italian
02 674 2020

For a taste of authentic Italy, Amalfi offers fresh pasta, risotto and seafood cooked to perfection by a Sicilian chef. The chic, Italian-inspired design (think Milan and the fashionistas), is open and airy, with big windows overlooking the terrace and pool. Traditional Italian music from the Sonata Duonello provides an excellent background to this stunning restaurant. The feel is unfussy, uncomplicated and simply elegant, lending itself to intimacy and romance. **Map** 2 F2

Amerigos
Park Inn Abu Dhabi, Yas Island

Mexican
02 656 2222

Suitable for casual or formal occasions, this spacious restaurant has a colourful, modern decor with a large TV at one end, dedicated mainly to sport. If you prefer, you can enjoy the view from the poolside dining area. Choose from traditional fajitas and quesadillas with fresh guacamole, or try meat and fish dishes, all well prepared and served by friendly staff. Alternatively, just sip a long cocktail at the bar. A bustling restaurant that almost always results in a lively, sociable evening. **Map** 1 H3

Amici > *p.IFC*
The Yas Hotel

Italian
02 656 0600

Amici has an almost futuristic vibe thanks to a large outside dining terrace, calming water features, moulded white furniture and green glass hanging sculptures. Fresh bread and a trio of flavoured olive oils start your meal delivered by staff who are attentive and helpful. While the menu is small (you choose from the antipasti buffet for your appetiser), every morsel is authentic and delicious. **Map** 1 H3

Angar > *p.IFC*
The Yas Hotel

Indian
02 656 0600

The smell of divine spices will lead you straight to Angar. Authentic tastes of India mix with contemporary luxury, served in one of the newest additions to Abu Dhabi's five star scene. Dine outside with views of the brightly coloured hotel dome, or inside where you can watch the chefs prepare your curries from scratch. Each course is carefully constructed and the extensive menu proves that variety really is the spice of life. **Map** 1 H3

Arabesque
InterContinental Al Ain Resort

International
03 768 6686

This top hotel buffet comes at a very affordable price. Served in spacious, attractive surroundings by polite and unobtrusive staff, the meal includes salads that are fresh and varied, and plenty of alternatives to the ubiquitous Lebanese mezze. Lunch is spiced up with a live cooking centre and evenings include a small set menu that complements the buffet. The desserts are definitely worth the drive. **Map** 4 H8

Asian Bistro & Sushi Bar
Abu Dhabi Golf Club

Japanese
02 558 8990

Set on the first floor of the Abu Dhabi Golf Club is this handy gem serving reasonably priced sushi. Try the chef's special for Dhs.85, which includes an assortment of 14 to 16 different pieces. On Monday evenings, enjoy a leisurely all-you-can-eat deal for only Dhs.105 per person. **Map** 1 F4

Assymetri
Radisson Blu Hotel, Abu Dhabi Yas Island

International
02 656 2000

Perfect for families with children, this restaurant is equipped with its own clown, toys and swimming pool. The international cuisine, by its very nature, caters for all and the live cooking stations make for dynamic entertainment. The large, bright interior also offers views over the Arabian Gulf. **Map** 1 H3

Bam Bu!
Abu Dhabi Marina & Yacht Club

Chinese
02 644 0300

Whether out for a romantic meal or a group dinner, you can't go wrong with Bam Bu! – a little slice of the Orient with an enchanting view of the yachts moored in the Marina. The set menu (Dhs.99, including unlimited selected beverages) is a good choice for the uninitiated – just relax while a stream of freshly prepared delicacies is brought to your table. **Map** 3 G3

Barouk
Crowne Plaza Yas Island

Arabic
02 656 3000

This recently opened Lebanese restaurant is ideal for travellers wanting an authentic taste of the Middle East. With a wide selection of hot and cold mezze, sharing is advisable in order to sample a range of the delights. Main course options are predominantly a choice of juicy lamb or chicken kebabs. Sweeten things up with the exquisite Turkish delight – a perfect accompaniment to the restaurant's own belly dancer who makes an appearance between 21:00 and 22:00, transforming the atmosphere from quiet and refined to lively and vibrant. **Map** 1 H3

Belgian Beer Café
Belgian
InterContinental Abu Dhabi
02 666 6888

A lively, European-style cafe setting with lots of noise and laughter coming from the bar. Tuck into some of the best fries in the city here, as well as pork cooked in a number of ways, but the specialty is steamed mussels in broths ranging from curry to white wine and tarragon. And it doesn't stop there – there are steaks, chicken and vegetarian selections to tantilise your tastebuds. All this, and the extensive choice of beers, have already made this a favourite among expats. **Map** 3 A3

Benihana
Japanese
Beach Rotana Abu Dhabi
02 644 3000

The gracious, contemporary Japanese cuisine, the minimalist decor and the crowd-pleasing teppanyaki chefs make this venue a must. The menu includes the usual soups, salads and desserts, but if it's Japanese you're after then don't miss out on the sushi and of course the teppanyaki, prepared at live cooking stations. Prices may seem high but for a feast of melt-in-your-mouth treats, it's good value. **Map** 3 G4

BiCE

Italian

Hilton Abu Dhabi

02 681 1900

For modern Italian cooking with a touch of romance, BiCE is a good choice. Low lighting and flickering candles on every table provide an intimate atmosphere while the decor is relaxed elegance. The hand-made pasta, and a good range of seafood dishes, are all prepared with care and presented with a flourish. It's Italian but with a twist on the traditional recipes such as the spaghetti with lobster bolognaise. **Map** 3 A2

Blue Grill Steakhouse

Steakhouse

Yas Island Rotana

02 656 4000

Elegant in shades of blue and dark wood, this restaurant, with its attentive staff, is light, airy and displays an extensive range of wine and an impressive show kitchen. Monday to Thursday, the restaurant offers an innovative a la carte menu, focusing on prime beef and seafood and, on Fridays, it hosts a truly sumptuous brunch. **Map** 1 H3

Bord Eau

French

Shangri-La Hotel Qaryat Al Beri

02 509 8888

Chef Gilles Perrin produces some gastronomic masterpieces, and the menu takes established luxuries – foie gras, scallops, lobster thermidor and Wagyu beef – and adds subtle twists. There is a hushed air of fine dining, and people come here for special occasions or for business (when someone else is picking up the tab). The service is faultless, but dinner for two will leave a considerable hole in your wallet. One of Abu Dhabi's finest. **Map** 2 D2

Caravan

Asian

Al Hamed Centre   02 639 3370

For a cheap, no-frills Asian meal, Caravan certainly delivers the goods. The menu offers a tasty selection of Chinese, Indian and Thai cuisine, and the great value for money evening buffet includes soups, salads, a selection of main courses and desserts. The service is remarkably friendly and helpful given that this is a low-cost venue. **Map** 3 E4

Casa Romana

Italian

Hilton Al Ain   03 768 6666

The well-known Casa Romana, overlooking the bustling lobby of the hotel, has an extensive menu of authentic Italian dishes, all generously portioned and delicious. Expect to find all your Italian favourites here, including pizza, pasta and a rather tasty seafood risotto. The decor evokes the feel of a rustic country terrace. **Map** 4 H8

Chamas Brazilian Churrascaria
Restaurant & Bar

Brazilian

InterContinental Abu Dhabi   02 666 6888

The concept is simple – all the red meat you can eat for a fixed price. The meat is fantastic and the salad bar is large enough to appease any vegetarians you may be dining with. All of it is included in the price. Be careful when ordering, however, as drinks and desserts aren't included. This noisy, frantic place with its enthusiastic band, is great for large groups and is packed every night, proving that Chamas has got the formula for Brazilian churrascaria just right. **Map** 3 A3

Chili's
Grand Al Mariah Cineplex

Tex-Mex
02 671 6300

It's not just the food that will attract you to Chili's. The enticing Tex-Mex menu brimming with juicy steaks, spicy chicken and lots of cheese and refried beans is certainly reason enough to go, and the super helpful service and family friendly atmosphere keeps punters coming back. Prices may seem high for a casual family restaurant, but the quality is superb. 'Guilt free' menu options will please the health conscious. **Map** 3 F2

Cho Gao > *p.243*
Crowne Plaza

Asian
02 621 0000

Cho Gao's menu reads like a food travelogue – an ingredient from China, a recipe from Thailand, a technique from Vietnam; salad, soup, dim sum. Recommended are the steak, duck and seafood options, while you'll also find some of the most creative vegetarian dishes in town. The ambience is calm and the decor authentic, while the service is attentive without being intrusive and the bar, with its two-for-one happy hour, is great for a quick drink and a snack after work. **Map** 3 F3

Ciro's Pomodoro
Al Diar Capital Hotel

Italian
02 678 7700

If you can't resist a charming Italian, then this venue is perfect. The menu covers all the classics like pastas, pizzas and grilled dishes, and the numerous pictures of celebrities visiting Ciro's around the world will keep you entertained. The food is delectable, the service friendly, and most evenings there's a live band to serenade you through your meal. **Map** 3 G2

Coconut Bay
Mongolian

Hilton Abu Dhabi   02 681 1900

The a la carte menu at Coconut Bay is impressive, but during the cooler months the Mongolian barbecue on Friday evenings is a hands-down winner. The extensive selection of sandwiches and the original salads make this a great place to recharge after a hard day's relaxing on the beach – the setting is ideal for a casual dinner and a few sundowners. There's also a special kids' menu that's sure to please. **Map** 3 A2

Eden Rock
Arabic

Mercure Grand Jebel Hafeet   03 783 8888

Location is everything (or so estate agents say) and the half-hour drive up Jebel Hafeet mountain for a spectacular view, and temperatures six to eight degrees cooler, make this well worth the trip. Sit on the terrace at night to get a dramatic sense of place, sample a standard Arabic buffet until 22:00 and carry on with a shisha until 02:00, while taking in a 180° vista of the Al Ain lights twinkling below.

El Sombrero
Tex-Mex

Sheraton Abu Dhabi Hotel & Resort   02 677 3333

Whether you're out for a relaxed dinner for two or a raucous night with your amigos, El Sombrero comes highly recommended. Fascinating Mexican artefacts and well thought out decor set the scene, while the food and the service both score highly. This lively venue is good on any night of the week but particularly worth checking out are the theme nights on Tuesdays and Wednesdays. **Map** 3 F2

Elements > *p.231*

International

Fairmont Bab Al Bahr

02 654 3333

This diverse all-day dining restaurant offers a variety of international choices. Taking on a buffet style, Elements has five live cooking stations and a cool, contemporary ambiance – there is also a popular outdoor eating area. Arabic and Indian dishes excel, the sushi is extremely good too and the dessert station is big enough to get lost in. It's worth booking as is it can get busy. **Map** 2 D1

Filini

Italian

Radisson Blu Hotel, Yas Island

02 656 2000

A spacious, modern restaurant where warming beiges, creams and dark woods calm the senses, if the weather allows, the terrace is an equally peaceful dining space. Filini is unashamedly Italian and the classic selection of pizza, fish, meat and pasta are done very well. The wine, service and presentation are excellent and the bar is perfect for a quiet chat over a deep claret. **Map** 1 H3

Finz

Seafood

Beach Rotana Abu Dhabi

02 697 9000

Sitting well apart from the other restaurants at the Beach Rotana, patrons might get the feeling that they're on something of a seafood pilgrimage. The restaurant's ample menu doesn't disappoint – from lobster to sea bass, and huge prawns, this place will keep you salivating. It's not cheap, but it's worth it for the oysters on the half shell alone. Attentive service and a gorgeous terrace setting (though marred by the

Clockwise from top left: El Sombrero, Elements, Cho Gao

construction on Sowwah Island) can turn a Monday night into an evening fit for a holiday. **Map** 3 G4

Gardinia
Al Ain Rotana Hotel

Mediterranean

03 754 5111

Live piano music fills the air while a carved ice swan presides over an array of fresh seafood laid out in a wooden dhow – welcome to Gardinia. This venue is popular throughout the week and reservations are a necessity. Seafood lovers won't know where to start but the seafood chowder is recommended and the red snapper is a treat. As for the desserts, if you have room then you won't be disappointed. **Map** 4 G8

Gerard Patisserie
Marina Mall

Cafe

02 681 4642

Located at the top of the escalators in this busy mall, Gerard is a great venue for people watching and a quick pitstop during a shopping spree. The simple menu offers light meals such as sandwiches and salads, and of course there is a good selection of pastries and both hot and cold beverages. The service is friendly and efficient. **Map** 3 B1

Havana Café
Nr Marina Mall

Cafe

02 681 0044

Situated in one of the finest locations in Abu Dhabi, Havana Café has stunning views that encourage relaxed alfresco dining during the cooler months. The international menu has something for everyone, and while breakfast and lunch are fairly quiet affairs, Havana transforms into a vibrant dinner venue in the evening. The service is courteous, and a 'shisha man' in traditional costume is an added attraction. **Map** 3 B1

Heroes > *p.243*

Crowne Plaza

American

02 621 0000

Arguably the city's best sports bar, Heroes is nearly always heaving with frenzied fans who come to watch the game in the company of similarly sports-mad folk. The familiar pub fare is tasty and portions are generous. Thankfully, the table service is friendly and surprisingly efficient, so there is no need to wrestle your way through the crowds just to get to the bar. Regular events such as Ladies Night, Quiz Night and Dance Night pack even more punters in. **Map** 3 F3

Hoi An

Shangri-La Hotel Qaryat Al Beri

Vietnamese

02 509 8888

The comprehensive menu comprises traditional Vietnamese favourites and delicious originals, such as kobe steak in a rich foie gras sauce. The staff are friendly and accommodating, tailoring dishes to suit the palates of chili lovers and loathers alike. Subtly decorated in a far eastern style indoors, the outdoor tables overlook the Al Maqta area and offer a more secluded dining experience. **Map** 2 D2

Idioms

Corniche Road West

Cafe

02 681 0808

This trendy yet unpretentious 'new kid on the block' has an interesting menu, friendly staff and a good location (near the Corniche in Khalidiya). The menu includes salads, sandwiches and some rather tasty pastas and main dishes. The signature espresso cocktails, served in shot glasses – a 'sweet swiss' or a 'sweet afro' – add a unique finish to a pleasant dining experience, and shouldn't be missed. **Map** 3 C2

Il Paradiso

Seafood

Sheraton Abu Dhabi Hotel & Resort   02 677 3333

Offering one of the capital's most scenic outdoor dining experiences, this is a leading player in Abu Dhabi's competitive seafood scene. Seafood lovers will not be disappointed by the range of fish and shellfish, all of which are imaginatively presented. It's not cheap (watch out for the 'cooking charge') but the food is good and the service friendly and efficient. **Map** 3 F2

Il Porto

International

Nr Marina Villages, Mirage Marine Complex   02 635 9957

Soft launched at the end of last year, Il Porto has now officially opened at the Mirage Marine complex. The restaurant features a stylish interior that is eclipsed by the outdoor terrace with views over blue waters to Emirates Palace. On offer is an intriguing mix of contemporary Italian fare and sushi (which feels a little affected, but just about works). Food and service are simple and fine and dishes are mouth-watering, but this very good restaurant is further elevated by its location. With a Lebanese restaurant, shisha garden and cafe also serving up treats, Mirage Marine is fast becoming an essential hangout (so long as booze isn't all you look for on a menu). **Map** 3 B1

Il Paradiso

India Palace

Indian
Opp ADNOC, Al Salam St   02 644 8777

This unassuming restaurant features an extensive menu and is generally busy. The food is tasty and at times pretty fiery, and portions are generous, offering good value for your dirham. Those with more delicate palates can request milder versions of their favourites. Quick, courteous waiters will patiently guide you through the menu if you are not an expert on North Indian Cuisine. **Map** 3 F3

Jing Asia

Asian
Crowne Plaza Yas Island   02 656 3000

Contemporary and colourful on the inside, with a rejuvenating sea view from the outside, the ambience at Jing Asia is impressive either way. Attentive, friendly staff prepare

fresh ingredients in the open kitchen which hosts traditional Asian cuisine, from sushi to stir fries; Friday brunch casts the net wider, even boasting a traditional roast with Yorkshire puddings. Ideal for large groups or parties, there is a variety of themed nights throughout the week. **Map** 1 H3

Kazu > *p.IFC*
The Yas Hotel

Japanese
02 656 0600

Kazu makes that difficult leap beyond Abu Dhabi's spectacular offerings to offer something truly special. The interior is simple, modern and nicely lit, but the terrace overlooking the Yas Marina and the race circuit makes for a unique backdrop to a social restaurant. Head chef Yu Cao trained under Nobu Matsuhisa, but it's possible that he has eclipsed his master's Dubai offering. The exceptional lightness and clarity of flavours almost defies belief, with the cucumber and seafood salad, shrimp and cream cheese sushi and teppanyaki particularly special. Wash it down with a Japanese beer or some sake. The presentation is excellent and to say the service is as good as the food is high praise indeed. **Map** 1 H3

Kwality
Al Salam Street

Indian
02 672 7337

If you like authentic Indian food at a very reasonable price, then Kwality is one of the best options in town. From North Indian Tandoori dishes to Goan curries, Kwality provides a wonderful tour through Indian cuisine. The food, service, and welcoming atmosphere make this one of the 'must do' Indian restaurants in the capital. **Map** 3 G2

La Brioche
Marina Mall

Cafe

02 681 5531

The extensive, reasonably priced menu at this charming bistro includes croissants, sandwiches, pizzas and soups, but also has a sweet and savoury crepes, some interesting fruit cocktails and several speciality hot drinks. **Map** 3 B1

La Mamma
Sheraton Abu Dhabi Hotel & Resort

Italian

02 677 3333

This spacious, well-appointed restaurant is an excellent choice for a romantic evening, a fun family feast or a respectable business meal. With the exception of the exotic antipasto buffet, the food is fairly standard but is well prepared and of good quality, from quick and filling pizzas to delicious and generous helpings of pasta and seafood. **Map** 3 F2

La Veranda
Sheraton Khalidiya Hotel

Buffet

02 666 6220

An upscale hotel restaurant with daily theme nights and good quality buffet fare to tempt everyone. It is a challenge to leave this restaurant feeling hungry as there is something delicious to suit all tastes. The dessert table is especially enticing so make sure you leave room. The decor is stylish and upmarket, and the service friendly and attentive. **Map** 3 D3

Le Beaujolais
Novotel Centre Hotel

French

02 633 3555

With its red-checked tablecloths and French-speaking, glass-clinking clientele, Le Beaujolais virtually transports you to a charming little bistro in Paris. The menu offers seafood and meat dishes, rounded off with a dessert selection including crackly crusted crème brulee. A daily set menu is also available. The service, headed by a friendly maitre d', is welcoming and attentive, but never obtrusive. **Map** 3 E3

Le Belvedere   International
Mercure Grand Jebel Hafeet   03 783 8888

Perched atop Jebel Hafeet, Le Belvedere has a wonderful (yet restricted) view over Al Ain. Serving both buffet and a la carte meals, the international cuisine has a clear Mediterranean influence. The Friday seafood buffet is well worth the drive, but perhaps the best way to experience Le Belvedere is to spend a night at the hotel, and enjoy the full package.

Le Bistrot   French
Le Meridien Abu Dhabi   02 644 6666

Connoisseurs of fine wines and elegant French cuisine will enjoy a superb culinary experience at Le Bistro in Le Meridien. In cooler months, the terrace offers a great opportunity to people watch while feasting on some top quality fare. The menu is a little limited but fans of simple fish and meat dishes prepared in a classic French style will be more than happy. Cheap it ain't, but you get what you pay for. **Map** 3 G3

Le Boulanger   Cafe
Bhs Building, Shk Hamdan Bin Mohd St   02 631 8115

This busy French cafe in the heart of the city is a great place to enjoy a European style breakfast, good coffee and a leisurely

Jing Asia

browse through the daily newspapers from around the world.
The menu is extensive, featuring tasty food in generous
quantities. There is a bakery counter selling the freshest
breads, croissants, tarts and cakes, which can be eaten on the
premises or taken home to enjoy later (or both!). **Map** 3 F3

Lebanese Flower
Nr Choithram, Khalidiya

Arabic
02 665 8700

This popular restaurant has a range of high quality grilled
meats and fish accompanied by delicious freshly baked
Arabic bread. A selection of Middle Eastern curries and meat
dishes are available at lunchtime. Service is super efficient –
the slightest nod of your head will instantly bring a bevy of
enthusiastic waiters to your table. **Map** 3 C3

Marakesh
Millennium Hotel Abu Dhabi

Moroccan
02 614 6000

Despite its elaborate decor, Marakesh has a fairly casual
ambience where exotic and delectable Moroccan food
(with more than a hint of Lebanese influence) is served in
generous portions by highly efficient waiters. A live band
adds atmosphere, and later in the evening an eye-poppingly
beautiful belly dancer makes a dramatic appearance. **Map** 3 F2

Mawal
Hilton Abu Dhabi

Arabic
02 681 1900

An Arabian belly dancer and singer top the bill at Mahwal, but
the excellent food, colourful service and lively atmosphere
are enough draw in themselves. In addition to an exhaustive

range of hot and cold Lebanese mezze, is a selection of superb kebabs grilled to perfection, including a melting lamb shish. If you plan to stay for the show, reservations are essential as the place really comes alive later on. Although it is a bit pricey, this restaurant is worth every dirham for a Lebanese banquet and a full night's Arabic entertainment. **Map** 3 A2

Mezzaluna
Emirates Palace

Italian
02 690 7070

From the time the complementary breads and olives are placed in front of you, until the time you devour the last crumb of your wicked (but wonderful) dessert, your experience at Mezzaluna will be a guaranteed delight. The Italian head chef uses divine inspiration to create a host of beautifully presented dishes, including fresh pasta concoctions, seafood creations and meat dishes, many of which are surprisingly easy on the pocket. Stunning decor and an opulent atmosphere also please. **Map** 3 A2

Min Zaman
Al Ain Rotana Hotel

Arabic
03 754 5111

Once you manage to find this restaurant in the depths of the Rotana hotel (ask for directions at reception), you are in for a superb evening of regional food and entertainment. Hot and cold mezze head the menu, followed by the usual grilled meats and fish, while desserts and shisha are all enjoyed against a backdrop of live music, singing and belly dancing. It gets crowded on Thursday nights, so reservations are recommended. **Map** 4 G8

Nautilus > *p.IFC*   Seafood
The Yas Hotel   02 656 0600

The strong nautical theme prevails at this swanky restaurant, from the waiters outfits to the white and blue interior and, of course, the seafood menu. It isn't cheap, but the food is excellent, and the terrace view of Yas Marina is magical. The set menu (Dhs.1,000 for two with a bottle of wine) is a good choice and all dishes come in perfect proportions. **Map** 1 H3

Nihal Restaurant   Indian
Shk Zayed 2nd St, Nr Sands Htl   02 631 8088

This established Indian restaurant offers great curries at rock bottom prices, and the menu is extensive enough to tickle just about anyone's fancy. The fragrant spices of the subcontinent are all expertly blended into tasty traditional dishes, served up with the usual relishes, yoghurts and chutneys. If Indian food is not your favourite, there are also various Chinese dishes on offer. **Map** 3 F3

Noodle Box > *p.IFC*   Asian
The Yas Hotel   02 656 0600

Noodle Box is a chic, romantic venue with an outdoor terrace overlooking the Yas Marina and F1 track. The menu is simple, but expertly designed. From prawn cakes prepared with fresh chilies and lime leaves, to signature dim sum and the wok specialties, each dish hides a myriad of flavours. The well selected wine list and, particularly, the house specialty beer, Tsingtao, complement the cuisine perfectly and the service is impeccable. **Map** 1 H3

Clockwise from top left: Nautilus, Le Boulanger, The Noodle House

the
noodle house

Oceans
Le Royal Meridien Abu Dhabi

Seafood
02 674 2020

African masks and heavy wicker furniture decorate this excellent restaurant. Serving a range of Indian, Thai and Malay dishes, the menu is dominated by seafood. Low lighting and widely spaced tables offer a feeling of intimacy, though the tables are a little large for two people. The venue also offers terrace dining in the cooler weather. Attentive staff provide excellent service to match the terrific food. **Map** 3 F2

Palm Lounge
Le Royal Meridien Abu Dhabi

Cafe
02 674 2020

The timeless tradition of afternoon tea is perfectly executed here, with dainty finger sandwiches and plump scones served on fine bone china, while you gaze out over the gardens and the pianist plays softly in the background. If you wish to indulge, upgrade to the Royal traditional tea which includes a glass of chilled champagne. **Map** 3 F2

Panda Panda Chinese Restaurant
Al Istiqlal St, Nr Jashanmal

Chinese
02 633 9300

This contemporary eatery mixes modern and traditional oriental influences. The extensive menu caters equally well to vegetarians, seafood lovers and carnivores, with the hot and sour soup and the Schezuan beef both heartily recommended. Service is quick, attentive and enthusiastic, and if the prices seem a little high, remember that portions are usually generous enough to feed two. **Map** 3 E4

Pappagallo
Le Meridien Abu Dhabi

Italian
02 644 6666

Pappagallo is like a little slice of Tuscany right in the heart of the Le Meridien Culinary Village. The menu caters to most tastes, offering all the usual favourites of Italian cuisine, such as pastas and pizzas, as well as a wonderful antipasto buffet. Whether you dine alfresco or indoors, the food is good, the atmosphere pleasant, and the service satisfactory. **Map** 3 G3

Pearls & Caviar
Shangri-La Hotel Qaryat Al Beri

Mediterranean
02 509 8777

Inside this posh bar and restaurant it's a sleek world of black, white and chrome. Outside, one of the most inspiring views of the Sheikh Zayed Grand Mosque can be admired shimmering in the waters of the creek. The extensive menu offers a splendid seafood selection, including plenty of caviar. Prices and service reflect the luxury menu items and dinner for two will set you back around Dhs.1,200. **Map** 2 D2

Prego's
Beach Rotana Abu Dhabi

Italian
02 644 3000

Prego's boasts a large, airy interior and superb terrace overlooking the beach. The food is wonderful – in addition to the pizzas prepared in an authentic wood-fired oven, the menu has a selection of both classic and innovative pasta dishes, main courses and desserts. The venue is family friendly, but the comfortable spaces between tables make this a good choice for an intimate dinner too. **Map** 3 G4

Rangoli
Yas Island Rotana

Indian
02 656 4000

Rangoli's laidback vibe provides the perfect setting for its delicious buffet serving North and South Indian cuisine, that is fresh and attractive. Starters and mains intermingle; vegetable samosas and homemade chutneys sitting beside meat, fish and vegetable curries. Sweet lovers can choose from traditional desserts, including milky payas, sticky laddu, and exotic fruits. With a la carte options available and friendly staff, Rangoli offers a good value curry fix. **Map** 1 H3

Restaurant China
Novotel Centre Hotel

Chinese
02 633 3555

This restaurant has been dishing up yummy Chinese cuisine to its satisfied customers for over 20 years now, and it's still going strong. The food and service are both of consistently high standards, with the Peking duck and kung pao prawns worthy of a special mention. The authentic decor and directional lighting enhance the warm, welcoming ambience. **Map** 3 E3

Riviera
Opp Abu Dhabi Post Office, Tourist Club Area

Arabic
02 676 6615

This bright and airy cafe mixes a relaxed Mediterranean setting with typical Lebanese cuisine. The tasty mezze and freshly grilled dishes are recommended, and accompanied perfectly by piping hot Arabic bread, which is baked on the premises. You'll even find a few European specialities on the menu, just in case Lebanese food doesn't tickle your fancy. **Map** 3 G3

Spice up your life

Rock Bottom Café
Al Diar Capital Hotel

American
02 678 7700

Named after the Wall Street crash, this vibrant American diner
has a somewhat split personality – go early in the evening
to enjoy a quiet dinner, or hang around until later when the
live music starts and the pace becomes frenetic. The menu
features succulent steaks, sizzling seafood and innovative
salads, as well as a range of lighter snacks. **Map** 3 G2

Rodeo Grill
Beach Rotana Abu Dhabi

Steakhouse
02 644 3000

Part old English drawing room, part old American shooting
lodge, Rodeo Grill comes across all high-end Argentinean
ranch. Salads, seafood and even a few veggie options make it
on to the menu but the spotlight shines firmly on the fantastic
range of steak cuts, with the grade nine marble Wagyu and
the bison rib eye the stars of the show. Prices are certainly not
cheap, but this is a truly excellent restaurant. **Map** 3 G4

Sayad
Emirates Palace

Seafood
02 690 9000

As the flagship restaurant of the luxurious Emirates Palace
Hotel, you can expect the ultimate dining experience. This
superb restaurant offers a seasonal menu of fresh seafood
from across the globe. Select your own fish or lobster from
the tanks along the wall and it will be prepared to your exact
tastes, or opt for the five-course set menu which will give
you a taste of everything from sushi to the catch of the day.
Luxury touches like a cooling towel spritzed with jasmine add

Sayad

to the elegance and sophistication. A simply sublime dining option! **Map** 3 A2

Selections

International

InterContinental Abu Dhabi

02 666 6888

Few restaurants are more aptly named than Selections. Buffets and a few live cooking stations are the name of the game here, with the variety reflecting Lebanese, Asian and Mediterranean cuisine. Ideal for a business meeting during the week or family brunch at the weekend, the large, light restaurant looks out over the pool and the Arabian Gulf below. **Map** 3 A3

Sevilla > *p.117*
Al Raha Beach Hotel

Mediterranean
02 508 0555

Offering both a la carte and buffet dishes, the restaurant's food is excellent and is complemented by efficient and friendly service. The buffet options are available on Wednesdays, Thursdays and at Friday brunch. The beautifully decorated ceilings add a special touch to the warm, intimate interior, though for a stunning view, opt for a table on the terrace. **Map** 1 G4

Shang Palace
Shangri-La Hotel Qaryat Al Beri

Chinese
02 509 8888

Shang Palace's extensive menu covers Cantonese and Szechuan cuisine in addition to many non-Chinese items, and seafood features prominently. The atmosphere is great, the service faultless, the staff impeccably dressed, and the food superb. The breath-taking views from the romantic terrace are more than enough reason to come and linger for the evening in the large, solid chairs. **Map** 2 D2

Shuja Yacht
Le Royal Meridien Abu Dhabi

Dinner Cruise
02 674 2020

A two-hour cruise aboard this sleek vessel is a unique way to celebrate in style, have an intimate evening or socialise in a large group. Food is served buffet style, with lobster tails, prawns and crabs vying for a place on your plate along with lamb, chicken and a myriad of side dishes and from the lowliest deckhand to the captain, every staff member goes all out to ensure you have a memorable and impressive trip. **Map** 3 F2

Clockwise from top left: Spaccanapoli Ristorante, Shang Palace, Prego's

Soba

Japanese
02 674 2020

Le Royal Meridien Abu Dhabi

Bypassing this restaurant will mean missing out on a delightful culinary experience. The food is beautifully presented and delicious, and for non-sushi eaters there are a number of alternatives. Waiters are on hand to make helpful suggestions and the chefs are in plain sight, making intriguing viewing. The decor is minimalist and the seating does not encourage lingering. **Map** 3 F2

Sofra Bld

International
02 509 8888

Shangri-La Hotel Qaryat Al Beri

Any restaurant that can boast three chocolate fountains is worth a visit. Accompanying the fountains is a breathtaking array of intricate buffet cuisine covering all four corners of the globe, from fresh sushi to shawarma kebabs to parrot fish. The light and airy interior is less suited to intimate occasions, while the outside terrace provides a perfect vantage point for views of the neighbouring Sheikh Zayed Grand Mosque. **Map** 2 D2

Spaccanapoli Ristorante > *p.243*

Italian
02 621 0000

Crowne Plaza

This new Italian restaurant is focused squarely on Naples and, although thoroughly modern, it has plenty of rustic features which embrace the traditional quality of simple Italian fare. Treats such as baked aubergine with mozzarella get the meal off to an excellent start, and all the traditional main courses are represented. Try the veal escalope, the fresh fish or, if you're hungry, the metre-long pizza with up to four toppings.

The food is excellent, the prices reasonable and it is suitable for a romantic dinner or a livelier affair. **Map** 3 F3

Tanjore
InterContinental Al Ain Resort

Indian
03 768 6686

Tanjore is a curry lover's dream. The menu is varied enough to please the most demanding of tastes, and provides clear descriptions on what's hot, hotter, healthy and vegetarian. The rich atmosphere and surroundings complement the delicious and tantalising flavours, and the service is what you would expect from a five-star hotel. **Map** 4 H8

Teatro
Park Rotana Abu Dhabi

Japanese
02 657 3333

Teatro's eclectic decor creates a dramatic but informal atmosphere and is echoed by the huge show kitchen. Choose from an impressive a la carte menu, which covers a spectrum of east to west fine dining dishes. Service is absolutely impeccable and Teatro is fast becoming a firm favourite. **Map** 2 C1

The Alamo
Abu Dhabi Marina & Yacht Club

Tex-Mex
02 644 0300

This restaurant, with its cantina style atmosphere and typical Alamo memorabilia, is renowned for its frozen margaritas, succulent spare ribs and sizzling fajitas. An 'All You Can Eat' menu, inclusive of unlimited house beverages, is available Friday to Tuesday from 19:00 to 23:00. Friendly and polite staff and an entertaining Latino band complete the ingredients for a great fun night out. **Map** 3 G2

The Restaurant
The Club
International
02 673 1111

The softly lit, Roman-style interior is the perfect setting for a romantic evening. With its regular theme nights, The Club Restaurant offers a superb choice of cuisines, each as tasty as the next. The service is attentive and the prices reasonable. Reservations are required but make sure you and your date arrive together as mobile phones are banned. **Map** 1 C2

The Fishmarket
InterContinental Abu Dhabi
Seafood
02 666 6888

With the tropical island decor and the smiley service, diners will immediately realise this is no business-as-usual Abu Dhabi hotel restaurant. The extensive selection of fresh seafood, as well as a cartload of fresh vegetables, noodles and rice, customers choose the style of cooking (grilled, sautéed, fried); the kind of sauce (green curry, red curry, oyster sauce); and the accompaniments. Not for meat lovers, this place concentrates on seafood and lifts it to another level. **Map** 3 A3

The Garden Restaurant > *p.243*
Crowne Plaza
International
02 621 0000

This faux alfresco 'garden' venue is decorated with an abundance of plants and even has a waterfall. Theme nights cover the cuisines of the world, and every evening you'll find an impressive buffet designed to delight your taste buds. The Friday brunch is a popular family affair, with truckloads of tasty food and plenty of entertainment for the kids, so you can enjoy a long lunch with a variety of liquid refreshments. **Map** 3 F3

The Garden Restaurant

The Hut

Cafe

Nr Pizza Hut, Khalifa St

03 751 6526

If you long for the charm of the cafes of Europe, you may have found your home from home here. It offers an oasis of calm on the bustling Khalifa Street, with its warmly decorated interior and gentle ambience. Recommended for breakfasts and all-day snacks, the food is consistently pleasant and servings are generous. **Map** 1 C3

The Meat Co > *p.195*

Steakhouse

Souk Qaryat Al Beri

02 558 1713

The Meat Co is a deceptively large restaurant, covering two floors plus a big outdoor deck. The energy of the open kitchen spills out to the restaurant giving the place a frenetic atmosphere, making it popular with large groups. When not rushed, the service has a casualness that isn't reflected in the steep prices. The meat is the best reason for coming here, and the beef menu is temptingly large. **Map** 2 D1

The Noodle House > *p.195*

Chinese

Souk Qaryat Al Beri

02 558 1699

Views of the Souk Qaryat Al Beri, coupled with a wide selection for vegetarians, spice lovers and healthy eaters, will leave everyone satisfied. The zen ambience and oriental music make this modern slice of Asia ideal for any type of social gathering, although it's best suited to lunch with friends and family, or dinner before a night out. Service is speedy, the prices are crowd-pleasing and the quality is consistently high. **Map** 2 D1

THE One

Sheikh Zayed 1st Street

Cafe
02 681 6500

With soft lighting and smart furnishings, this cafe echoes the shop in which it's situated. There are three distinct menus depending on your mood: the 'Chic' menu is crammed with healthy options, 'Vogue' features traditional dishes including soups and salads, and 'Risque' is home to familiar dishes with an unexpected twist, such as Mexican falafel. Vegetarians will be particularly pleased with the selection on offer. **Map** 3 B3

The Village Club

One To One Hotel – The Village

Arabic
02 495 2000

The Village Club is situated amid a mature lawn with huge trees and scattered with tables and comfortable Arabic tents. At the buffet, starters include soup, mezze and salads, mixed freshly on request. From the barbecue, there's a variety of beef, lamb, chicken and fish, along with side dishes. Weekends are great for families, and in the evenings it is a great place to enjoy a calmer meal along with shisha or drinks. **Map** 3 F6

The Wok

InterContinental Al Ain Resort

Asian
03 768 6686

Staff members here are proud of their food, service and reputation, and with good reason – The Wok is one of the better restaurants serving Far Eastern cuisine in the area. Set in the landscaped grounds of the hotel, the ambience is quiet and relaxed with soft background music and stylish decor. The Wok is popular and reservations are essential, particularly for the outstanding seafood buffet on Sunday nights. **Map** 4 H8

Trader Vic's
Al Ain Rotana Hotel

Polynesian
03 754 5111

Forget the desert and spend an evening in tropical island mode at this popular Polynesian venue. The menu forgoes authentic Polynesian food, preferring instead to satisfy the cosmopolitan clientele with a delicious and diverse range of international dishes. The wine list is extensive, albeit somewhat overshadowed by the impressive list of cocktails, some of which are so potent they should carry a health warning. **Map** 4 G8

Trader Vic's
Beach Rotana Abu Dhabi

Polynesian
02 644 3000

Whether for business or pleasure, Trader Vic's is one of Abu Dhabi's long-standing favourite restaurants. The consistent quality of the food, the attentive staff and the relaxed tropical ambience keep people coming back time and time again. Try one of their world-famous cocktails as you peruse the exciting menu of tantalising French Polynesian dishes. **Map** 3 G4

Vasco's
Hilton Abu Dhabi

International
02 681 1900

Vasco's is a contemporary, fine dining venue offering a fusion of European, Arabic and Asian cuisines. Food is prepared to a very high standard and imaginatively presented. The patio offers a pleasant, alfresco setting, and as this is one of the more popular restaurants in Abu Dhabi, reservations are recommended whether for lunch and dinner. **Map** 3 A2

Clockwise from top left: Trader Vic's, The Wok, The Meat Co

Wasabi

Japanese

Al Diar Mina Hotel

02 678 1000

Enter the stark minimalism of the Wasabi interior for a light, healthy twist on Japanese cuisine – think fusion rather than authentic Japanese. The appetisers, including chicken dumplings, sushi and sashimi, are good value for money and are light enough to pave the way for a main course dish such as black bean noodles or teriyaki smoked salmon. The small selection of conventional wines should steer you towards the Japanese sake, served hot or cold. **Map** 3 G2

Zari Zardozi

Indian

Al Raha Mall

02 556 5188

The theme of Indian opulence, silk and spice is clearly reflected in Zari Zardozi with its rich red walls, copper ceiling and fragrant incense. Intimate seating arrangements add to the exotic mood. The north and south Indian menu is extensive, and the staff will happily discuss your spice preferences. Other options include fusion food, a diet menu and 'tandushi' – which combines tandoori and sushi. **Map** 1 G4

Zest

Cafe

The Club

. 02 673 1111

Zest is a haven for tea connoisseurs, with an exhaustive selection of teas to choose from and deep, comfy sofas to sink into while you sip on your favourite cuppa. Each cup of tea is accompanied by a mouthwatering homemade cookie, and there are newspapers and magazines to read, should your company be a little tedious. **Map** 1 C2

Vasco's

Zyara Café

Cafe

Corniche Rd West, Nr Hilton Residence

02 627 5006

Zyara in Arabic means 'visit,' and this trendy cafe definitely deserves one. The glass frontage offers a good view of the Corniche, and the laidback interior, with its rustic, Victorian style is an ideal meeting place. The quality and presentation of the food is excellent and the service is friendly and attentive, but all this does come at a price. **Map** 3 D1

Bars, Pubs & Clubs

There are a decent number of bars and clubs on offer in the city which range from uber-trendy cocktail lounges to jazz, cigar and champagne bars.

Captain's Arms
Le Meridien Abu Dhabi

Pub
02 644 6666

Overlooking the gardens, this tavern, with its cosy interior and upbeat outdoor terrace, offers the ambience of a traditional British pub. The daily happy hour (17:00 to 20:00), nightly entertainment, and food and drink specials bring in the crowds. Food portions are generous and generally satisfying, although you won't find many culinary surprises here. **Map** 3 G3

Cloud Nine – Cigar & Bottle Club
Sheraton Abu Dhabi Hotel & Resort

Cigar Bar
02 677 3333

From the first puff on your hand-picked Cohiba, Monte Cristo or Bolivar (delivered to you on a silver platter), to the last bit of Beluga passing your lips, this luxurious venue exudes a pleasing mix of old boys' charm and trendy sophistication. Service is pleasant and discreet, and a pianist adds further elegance to a classy (albeit smoky) evening out. **Map** 3 F2

Colosseum
Abu Dhabi Marina & Yacht Club

Club
02 644 0300

Visit this Roman-style nightclub any night of the week and rub shoulders with the young and hip on the snug, yet pumping, dance floor. The latest R&B and pop fusion beats, belted out by capable DJs, make this multicultural venue one of the city's favourite hotspots. As an added bonus, drinks are reasonably priced and ladies get in free. **Map** 3 G3

Cooper's

Pub

Park Rotana Abu Dhabi

02 657 3325

Cooper's could well become the next major hangout for Abu Dhabi expats. Not only will you find a friendly pint and some superb pub grub, but all major football matches are also shown here (call ahead for details). Cooper's offers 50% off selected beverages during its extended 'happy hour'. With its spacious interior and additional seating outside, it's great for informal gatherings. **Map** 2 C1

Cristal

Cigar Bar

Millennium Hotel Abu Dhabi

02 614 6000

Once the masterful bar manager has poured you a glass of champagne and helped you select the perfect smoke, you can sit back and relax in surroundings of polished wood, leather and subdued lighting. The tinkling tunes played by the in-house pianist make the perfect accompaniment, and if all this sophistication leaves you feeling peckish, a small range of tasty snacks is available. **Map** 3 F2

Havana Club

Bar

Emirates Palace

02 690 9000

In keeping with the grandeur of the hotel, the Havana Club exudes opulence and luxury while hinting at the personality of an 'old boys club' type exclusive bar. The bar area has the younger, more outgoing spirit, while the deep leather armchairs tucked in at the back are the personification of refinement. Relax and enjoy an exotic cocktail or maybe a vintage brandy, and snack on exquisitely presented canapes. You can even enjoy a fine Cuban cigar or cigarillo. The Havana club is open from 14:00 to 02:00 daily. **Map** 3 A2

Jazz Bar & Dining   Bar
Hilton Abu Dhabi   02 681 1900

For a relaxed evening of jazz, champagne and good food in a stylish setting, the Jazz Bar is worth a visit. Each dish on the extensive menu is available in two sizes – 'down beat' for the not so hungry, and 'main melody' for the ravenous. Special dietary needs can be met on request. As can be expected in any good bar, the wine list and drinks selection are impressive. The popular band keeps the rhythm alive and attracts a crowd, especially at weekends. **Map** 3 A2

LAB – Lounge At The Beach   Club
Beach Rotana Abu Dhabi   02 644 3000

Before 22:00, this is a sophisticated meeting place for those who want to chat. Arrive later if you'd rather party in a cross between a futuristic, all flashing nightspot and an Ibiza rave. In contrast to the loud but attractively lit bar area, the spacious terrace overlooking the beach is relaxed and welcoming. Not the cheapest drinking hole in town but certainly a stylish venue with potential for a good time. Don't be deceived by the refreshing taste of the cocktails as they're strong. **Map** 3 G4

PJ O'Reilly's

Pub

Le Royal Meridien Abu Dhabi   02 674 2020

This Irish pub is extremely popular, with a friendly and inviting atmosphere. The menu is pub grub with flair, with large portions and good value for money. The lively bar downstairs is the place to meet and greet, though you can escape to the quieter upstairs or alfresco dining areas. Big-screen TVs show sport, but the sound is generally only on during live football matches. Happy Hour runs from 12:00 to 20:00 every day, with other specials happening regularly through the week. **Map** 3 F2

Paco's
Bar

Hilton Al Ain   03 768 6666

Paco's has become somewhat of a living legend thanks to the fact that it never changes. Popular because it is exactly the same now as it was when it opened in 1991, this British watering hole is a tonic for the homesick expat's soul. After a steaming plate of bangers and mash, an excellent pint of Guinness (hard to come by in these parts) and a spot of footie on the big screen, you'll almost forget you are miles away from home. There's a daily happy hour between 12:00 and 20:00. **Map** 4 H8

Relax@12
Bar

Aloft Abu Dhabi   02 654 5000

Whether in the mood for after-work cocktails in the rooftop lounge or a casual meal alfresco, this spot hits the mark. The decor is decidedly modern with glowing bars, dim lighting and angular furniture, but both the terrace and the bar attract a refreshing mix of ages. The view alone is worth a visit, but with an extensive menu of beer, wine and cocktails, and a small but dependable menu of sushi and Japanese favorites, this is a perfect spot for making a night of it. **Map** 2 A2

SAX
Bar

Le Royal Meridien Abu Dhabi   02 674 2020

The chic set will love this restaurant's trendy, New York style. A live jazz band and a well-stocked bar contribute to the vibey atmosphere as you unwind on the comfortable sofas with one of the many exotic cocktails on offer. Like most trendy

eateries, the quality of the ingredients and presentation cannot be faulted, and special drink offers and free cocktails for ladies help to make the evening even more enjoyable.
Map 3 F2

Stills
Pub

Crowne Plaza Yas Island   02 656 3000

This lively bar serves the cool youth as well as the gracefully aged. There's a nice list of specialty cocktails and whiskeys, as well as several international beers on tap and a cigar humidor giving the impression that this bar is serious about fun. The gastro-pub menu serves everything from steaks and burgers to pan-seared salmon, while the picturesque terrace is perfect for the mild breezy nights. There's also a DJ pool party night once a month, and Stills serves as a sometime-stopover for touring bands. **Map** 1 H3

YBar
Bar

Yas Island Rotana, Abu Dhabi   02 656 4000

Sit inside on YBar's long wooden tables and watch sport on TV or, if the weather permits, choose the outside terrace which has ambient lighting, low seating, and overlooks the other Yas hotels. The extensive drinks menu focuses on cocktails and spirits with a decent list of beers and wine. The food menu, although small, provides tasty basics such as shepherds pie, and steak and chips along with a handful of bar snacks. Reggae tunes help create the bars informal atmosphere. **Map** 1 H3

Index

Live Work Explore Guides

All you need to know about living, working and enjoying life in these exciting destinations

Mini Visitors' Guides

Perfect pocket-sized visitors' guides

Activity Guides

Drive, trek, dive and swim... life will never
be boring again

EXPLORER

Mini Maps

Fit the city in your pocket

Maps

Never get lost again

Photography Books

Beautiful cities caught through the lens

Practical & Lifestyle Products & Calendars

The perfect accessories for a buzzing lifestyle

EXPLORER

Explorer Team
Check out www.explorerpublishing.com

Publishing
Founder & CEO Alistair MacKenzie
Associate Publisher Claire England

Editorial
Group Editor Jane Roberts
Editors Matt Warnock,
Siobhan Campbell
Deputy Editor Pamela Afram
Corporate Editor Charlie Scott
Production Coordinator
Kathryn Calderon
Senior Editorial Assistant
Mimi Stankova
Editorial Assistant Ingrid Cupido

Design
Creative Director Pete Maloney
Art Director Ieyad Charaf
Account Manager Chris Goldstraw
Designer Michael Estrada
Junior Designer Didith Hapiz
Layout Manager Jayde Fernandes
Layout Designers Mansoor Ahmed,
Shawn Zuzarte
Cartography Manager
Zainudheen Madathil
Cartographers Noushad Madathil,
Sunita Lakhiani
Traffic Manager Maricar Ong
Traffic Coordinator Amapola Castillo

Sales & Marketing
Group Media Sales Manager
Peter Saxby
Media Sales Area Managers
Laura Zuffa, Lisa Shaver, Pouneh Hafizi
Media Sales Executive Bryan Anes

Marketing & PR Manager
Annabel Clough
Marketing & PR Assistant
Shedan Ebona
Group Retail Sales Manager
Ivan Rodrigues
Senior Retail Sales Merchandisers
Ahmed Mainodin, Firos Khan
Retail Sales Merchandisers
Johny Mathew, Shan Kumar
Retail Sales Coordinator
Michelle Mascarenhas
Drivers Shabsir Madathil,
Najumudeen K.I.
Warehouse Assistant
Haji Mohamed Sarabudeen

Photography
Photography Manager Pamela Grist
Photographer Victor Romero
Image Editor Henry Hilos

Finance & Administration
Administration Manager
Shyrell Tamayo
Accountant Cherry Enriquez
Accounts Assistants Soumyah Rajesh,
Sunil Suvarna
Front Office Administrator
Janette Tamayo
Personnel Relations Officer Rafi Jamal
Office Assistant Shafeer Ahamed

IT & Digital Solutions
Digital Solutions Manager
Derrick Pereira
Senior IT Administrator R. Ajay
Web Developer Anas Abdul Latheef

Contact Us

▶ Register Online

Check out our new website for event listings, competitions and Dubai info, and submit your own restaurant reviews.
Log onto **www.liveworkexplore.com**

▶ Newsletter

Register online to receive Explorer's monthly newsletter and be first in line for our special offers and competitions.
Log onto **www.liveworkexplore.com**

▶ General Enquiries

We'd love to hear your thoughts and answer any questions you have about this book or any other Explorer product.
Contact us at **info@explorerpublishing.com**

▶ Careers

If you fancy yourself as an Explorer, send your CV (stating the position you're interested in) to **jobs@explorerpublishing.com**

▶ Designlab and Contract Publishing

For enquiries about Explorer's Contract Publishing arm and design services contact **designlab@explorerpublishing.com**

▶ Maps

For cartography enquries, including orders and comments, contact **maps@explorerpublishing.com**

▶ Media and Corporate Sales

For bulk sales and customisation options, for this book or any Explorer product, contact **sales@explorerpublishing.com**

Notes

Notes